Arthur Douglass

**Ostrich Farming in South Africa**

Being an Account of its Origin and Rise

Arthur Douglass

**Ostrich Farming in South Africa**
*Being an Account of its Origin and Rise*

ISBN/EAN: 9783337307677

Printed in Europe, USA, Canada, Australia, Japan

Cover: Foto ©ninafisch / pixelio.de

More available books at **www.hansebooks.com**

# OSTRICH FARMING

IN

# SOUTH AFRICA.

BEING AN ACCOUNT OF

*Its Origin and Rise; How to set about it;*
*The Profits to be derived; How to Manage the Birds;*
*The Capital required; the Diseases and Difficulties*
*to be met with, &c. &c.*

BY

## ARTHUR DOUGLASS,

*Inventor and Patentee of the "Eclipse" and other Ostrich Incubators; Medallist of the*
*Société d'Acclimatation, Paris International Exhibitions, &c.*

CASSELL, PETTER, GALPIN & CO.,
*LONDON, PARIS & NEW YORK;*
AND
S. W. SILVER & CO., SUN COURT, 67, CORNHILL, LONDON, E.C.

# PREFACE.

In undertaking to write on "Ostrich Farming in South Africa," I have done so at the urgent solicitations of friends, and in response to the numerous letters addressed to me from all parts of the world asking if any such work were to be had. In presenting it to the public, I do so knowing that many imperfections will be found. As a literary production, written at broken intervals in the midst of a busy life, it is necessarily far from perfect. As the first work of its kind ever published, it is no doubt far from exhaustive; but, such as it is, we present it to our fellow-colonists, intending emigrants, and others, as an honest attempt to help others on the road we have travelled ourselves, and to forward the best interests of the Colony of our adoption and affection.

ROYAL COLONIAL INSTITUTE,
15, STRAND, LONDON.
*June* 22, 1881.

# CONTENTS.

## ILLUSTRATIONS.

# OSTRICH-FARMING IN SOUTH AFRICA.

IN treating of Ostrich-farming it is essential to bear in mind what a short time has elapsed since the first domestication of the wild bird, which we can only date back about fourteen years; as, although previous to this a few Ostriches had been kept in zoological gardens, and in parks, like that of the late Sir Walter Currie, at Oatlands Park, Grahamstown, we have not heard that any one had them breeding in a tame state. So that, although we should have to go back a long period to find when the first tamed Ostrich was kept, the domestication of Ostriches for the purpose of farming them for the sake of their plumage must be taken to date from 1867. As to who should bear the palm for being the first to have succeeded in domesticating the Ostrich, i.e., to have had a nest from tamed birds, and to have reared their chicks in a tame state, it may be hard to decide. We believe some challenge our claim:

B

whether justly or not, we cannot say; at any rate, we believe no one disputes that we were the first to make it our sole occupation, and to bring it before the world as the extraordinarily lucrative and great industry it has now become— an industry in which in the Cape Colony alone there is not less than £8,000,000 of capital employed, and with an export of feathers for last year of 163,065 lbs. weight, valued at £883,632, being equal to £5 8s. 4d. per lb., the great mass of which was from tame birds. It seems almost unaccountable that for over forty years after the landing of the British settlers in the colony such a mine of wealth should have lain at their doors, within almost daily sight of them, as at that time the wild bird was in abundance throughout Albany, and right up to the Zambesi, and many of the most adventurous of the settlers made an occupation of hunting the birds and exporting the feathers, and constantly came upon broods of young birds; or even later on, when the birds were destroyed and hunted into more inland parts, and Grahamstown became the main centre from which the traders fitted out and returned to sell their feathers, and the inhabitants constantly saw feathers sold for nearly their weight in gold, yet the idea never struck them of domesticating the bird, and reaping a half-yearly crop of feathers, instead of shooting it for a single crop.

The consideration of this should act as a great stimulus to every young man to keep his eyes open for other mines of wealth, which no doubt lie around us in this, as yet, little-developed land. But any one who will discover these must rely entirely on himself, and must not be deterred by any amount of sneers and ridicule. Many a time at first we were told we were mad, and should leave it alone; that it would never pay; that the birds were naturally of so timid a nature, they would never breed in confinement; or if they ever did make a nest, that it was their nature to break all their eggs if any one went near it; and that even if all other difficulties were overcome, the feather grown in a tame state would not curl, and would be of little value. This latter was extensively believed, even by the dealers in feathers, and for some years a great prejudice was maintained against tame feathers. As this has quite died out now, it is hard to account for it, and only shows how strong prejudice is against anything new.

The French have made great efforts to introduce Ostrich-farming in Algiers, but it does not seem to have taken much root there. Birds are also, to a small degree, kept in a tame state in Egypt. But South Africa has become, and is likely to remain, the great seat of the industry.

B 2

The Melbourne Acclimatisation Society imported some into Australia about eight years ago, but they have only slightly increased, and the experiment as yet can hardly be considered a success. A few other small lots have also been introduced into some of the other Australian colonies.

Last year a shipment of over a hundred birds took place from Cape Town to Buenos Ayres.

The North African Ostrich is considered to give a more valuable feather than the South African, and a few years ago two pairs of birds were imported at Port Elizabeth from Barbary.

For some years not only farmers, but experienced business men, were always prognosticating that the feather market would collapse with the increase of the Ostrich; but the reverse has been the case. Fourteen years ago the export of feathers from the Cape was only valued at £70,000, entirely from wild birds, and yet prices were no higher than they are now, and the fluctuations of price have not been so great as in most other staple raw productions. One of its great safeguards is, that it is part of the Court dress; and as long as it is so it will always be fashionable; and the vested interests, not only of the growers, but, what is more important, of wealthy men in Europe, in the shape of the manufacturers of the curled and dressed feather, and of the dealers, is so great that no fear need be entertained of its being allowed to go out of fashion. Besides which, the feather is undoubtedly the most beautiful article of ornament of its kind, and as such is independent of fashion to a great extent.

Other markets are opening for them, creating at this time a greater demand than the present increase of birds can supply. The last quarter's customs returns show an export to the United States of America—a totally new market for us—of £12,000 worth, whilst we personally have received large orders for another new market.

# CHAPTER II.

## THE OSTRICH.

THE Ostrich family is represented by four species, viz., the Ostrich proper (*Struthio camelus*), the Rhea, the Emu, and the Cassowary. Some naturalists give a fifth, viz., the Apteryx, inhabiting New Zealand; but this we consider a mistake, as, although it possesses many of the characteristics of the Ostrich, it differs from them so much in other respects as to exclude it from the family.

The family differs from other birds in having only rudimentary wings, unadapted to flight; in having the barbs of the feathers of equal length on each side of the quill, and of such a nature as to deprive it of the means of flight, and in having the breast rounded like a barrel, instead of being like a keel, as in birds of flight.

### THE OSTRICH PROPER

is distinguished from the other members of the family—

(1.) By being the only one with two toes:

(2.) By being twice the size of the others:

(3.) By its eggs averaging upwards of three pounds

in weight, whilst the others barely average one and a quarter pound :

(4.) By the head and neck being bare of feathers :

(5.) By the beauty of its plumage, the only other member of the family producing feathers of any marketable value being the Rhea.

It is indigenous to and inhabits the whole continent of Africa and Arabia, but in the latter it is now nearly extinct.

The Rhea, or South American Ostrich, has three toes and no tail, and produces feathers somewhat similar to the chicken feathers of the Ostrich proper. They are known in the trade as "vantour" or vulture feathers, being worth from 4s. to 30s. a pound. A curious case of swindling came to light last year in Port Elizabeth, where a man, largely engaged in the feather trade, imported large quantities of these feathers, and mixing them up with the inferior kinds of white and grey Ostrich feathers, sold them again as Ostrich feathers at an enormous profit, completely deceiving the colonial buyers, the matter not being discovered till the feathers got into the hands of the London manufacturers.

The Rhea inhabits, in vast numbers, that part of South America which lies south of the Equator and east of the Andes mountains, extending down to the Straits of Magellan, thus reaching to 18 degrees nearer the Pole than the Ostrich. It is being rapidly destroyed for the sake of its feathers, which are being exported in enormous quantities, principally to North America and France. The egg of the Rhea, like the Ostrich, is cream-coloured when fresh laid, gradually turning quite white.

### THE EMU

inhabits the whole of Australia, and Australia only. It has three toes, is of a brown colour, the feathers being of a crisp, hairy nature, and of no commercial value. Its eggs are very handsome, being of a deep blue colour, and much indented. It has all the habits of the Ostrich. The plumage of the two sexes is of the same colour. It is fast being destroyed, as the country gets filled up with sheep.

### THE CASSOWARY

is found sparsely in Northern Australia, some parts of the Malay Archipelago, and in the South Pacific. It is distinguished from the other members of the Ostrich family by a large horny excrescence on its head, and most of the species, of which there are several, have one or two wattles suspended from the neck. It stands, like the Emu, about five feet high, is of a very dark brown colour, has hairy feathers of no value, is quite wingless, and lays a light-greenish egg.

The whole tribe are noted for their excessive shyness and timidity, without which in the struggle for existence in the world they would ere this have ceased to exist, from being deprived of the powers of flight.

We have taken this glance at the other members of the family, as it is essential that the Ostrich-farmer should know thus much of them ; but we shall not have again to refer to them, as our remarks will be entirely on the African Ostrich (*Struthio camelus*), so called from the resemblance of its foot to that of the camel. We will now take a glance at its anatomy.

The reader need not fear a lot of dry, hard, scientific names that would convey no information to him. My intention is to convey such a general knowledge of the frame of the bird the Ostrich-farmer has to deal with, as shall assist him to make post-mortems of birds that may die, and to convey in an intelligent manner to other farmers anything peculiar he may notice.

### THE LEG.

Most farmers call the joints by their wrong names. The Ostrich walks on its toes ; what is commonly called the ankle-joint is the second toe-joint of man. The so-called knee-joint corresponds with the ankle-joint, and

the so-called thigh, where we brand, with the calf; the
proper thigh being the short thick bone above this.
This is the usual formation of all swift-footed animals,
the part from what most farmers call the knee down-
wards being the foot, the heel being exceedingly long.
It is very advisable that farmers should remember this,
so that in describing to each other malformation or
injuries, there should be no confusion; so we have—

1st. The first toe-joint;

2nd. The second toe-joint;

3rd. The ankle-joint;

4th. The knee-joint, above the place we brand;

5th. The thigh-joint.

The leg is easily broken, either with a blow or when
they are dancing, when there is nothing for it but to
kill them.    They are also subject to spraining the ankle-
joint and instep, for which the best remedy is cold water
bathing and arnica lotion.    We have had them put the
ankle-joint completely out; if seen to at once this can
be easily pulled in, and a few hours' cold bathing and
leaving them in a dark stable, so that they do not use
the leg, will put them all right in a couple of days.
They will sometimes get tumours on the leg; these
are easily opened and removed, when the place should
be well cauterised.    Young birds will sometimes get a
staggering gait, knocking the legs together as they

walk; this is the after-effect of the birds having eaten some poison, and although they may live for a long time they will gradually get worse and die.

## THE WING,

which constitutes nearly the whole value of the bird, is exceedingly small, and the feathers are unadapted for flight, but in other respects it is perfect.

They are rather subject, especially as young birds, to put out the first or small joint, which is known by the wing hanging down. It is easily pulled into place, and should be at once tied to the other wing over the back, and left, when it will soon get right again.

## THE HEAD

is exceedingly small, and consequently the brain is small also. This has been calculated to be in the proportion of 1 to 1,200 as compared with its whole body, whilst the eagle's is as 1 to 160, and the parroquet's as 1 to 45; and yet the bird is anything but stupid, as every man must own who has seen it breaking open the shell to let out a chick that is fast inside, or has seen it managing its chicks. The eye is the only organ of the head we have known subject to disease. In all cases there is nothing like pouring in a lotion of sulphate of zinc, and repeating it constantly—as much as will lie on a shilling to a quart bottle of water is the strength required. We have known ants to attack little chicks, and nearly blind a whole brood, which were all saved with this treatment.

### THE NECK

is remarkable for its great length and for its formation, allowing the bird to turn its head completely round. They are very apt to get bones stuck fast in swallowing; if they cannot be forced up again, an incision should be made, the bone removed, and the place sewn up, when it will quickly heal.

### THE HEART

lies immediately under the junction of the neck with the body. They are very subject to dropsy of this organ, or what is commonly known as water on the heart, which will be treated of when considering worms.

### THE LUNGS

lie along the back-bone, extending down the ribs, but not adhering to them. They should be of a beautiful vermilion colour. When diseased or congested, it will be known by their black appearance, and by the clotted blood found inside.

### THE LIVER

comes immediately behind the heart. There is no gall bladder. In health it is of a deep plum colour, with a beautiful flush on it, and is remarkable for its inviting look.

These constitute the organs protected by the ribs, and are separated from the remaining organs by a diaphragm across the body. Continuing our course from head to tail, we next have

### THE GIZZARD,

or the mill where the food is ground up. This should always be hard and full of stones. It is subject in disease to get flabby, and consequently to allow the stones to pass into the intestines and out in the dung, as they should never do if the bird is in health. But more of this in treating of worms.

### THE STOMACH

is the organ into which the food passes at once when swallowed. It corresponds with the crop of other birds. It is here that the juices are given out to the food from small cells dotted over a portion of the stomach, and it is the seat of one of the most formidable diseases that has yet appeared (*See* WORMS). From the stomach the food passes up into the gizzard, and from thence into the intestines. The stomach and the gizzard are united together, and held by a diaphragm to the left side of the bird, to the left side of the backbone, and to the diaphragm, which divides the body in two. Thus the right side of the body, when the stomach is empty, has in it only the first small entrail; when the stomach is full, it extends nearly from side to side. These are points that must be borne in mind when we come to consider caponising.

### THE INTESTINES.

These are roughly divided into the small and large intestines, or otherwise the upper and lower. The small intestines extend from the gizzard to the " cœca " (otherwise known as the two blind stomachs, from their having no outlet). In the small intestines the food is converted into what is called chyle. It is here we find the Tape-worm. From the " cœca " the large intestines begin. First we have the maniply, or what corresponds in cattle and sheep to the book paunch. From the maniply we pass on down the large intestines to the rectum. It is in these latter that we get constipation, or stop sickness, which is so fatal to the Ostrich.

## THE TESTICLES

of the male, or the ovarium of the female, lie opposite the stomach, and under the hump in the back-bone,
to which they are suspended.

## THE KIDNEYS

are exceedingly large, extending along the back-bone
from the testicles to the bladder.

## THE BLADDER

lies just below the rectum, and is nothing more
than an enlargement of the extreme end of the intestines.

The penis is curled up in the bladder.

The bones of the Ostrich, as in other birds, are
hollow.

The age to which an Ostrich can live is unknown.
It has been usually supposed to be very great, possibly
a hundred years, as some people assert, though we
believe this to be entirely guess-work. The usual calculation for animals, that of six times the period it takes
to arrive at maturity, would give it twenty-four years,
but we are inclined to think that it reaches a greater
age than this.

# CHAPTER III.

WITH a new industry like Ostrich-farming it is highly essential to bear in mind the past history of the country in regard to its stock-carrying capabilities, and, if possible, so to manage things as to avoid all the ills that have befallen the other great industry of wool-growing.

The great body of the Cape Colony consists of great plains of Karoo country, composed of exceedingly fertile soil covered with alkaline bushes, with a scant and uncertain rainfall, in which cultivation is impossible without irrigation. The rainfall gradually gets less and less to the north-west, until in Namaqua Land we have a rainless country. The Karoo country is exceedingly good for sheep-walks, the sheep keeping in better health, increasing more rapidly, and growing larger than in other parts, and all other kinds of stock thrive better than in the grass country. But it is occasionally subject to such terrible droughts that heavy losses in stock occur.

On the coast, and extending on an average about thirty miles inland, is a heavy, sour grass country, on

which stock will not thrive and sheep will not live at all. Cattle, unless bred on it, die to an immense extent of liver complaints; only a small percentage of the calves can be reared. Horses get poor and wretched. The veldt swarms with myriads of ticks—from the little fellow that burrows in the skin of man, producing horrid sores, to the large Bonte tick that destroys the teats of the cows, and produces terrible sores on all animals. But it has a fine and comparatively certain rainfall of over thirty inches annually, and cultivation is carried on to a large extent without any irrigation, the crops never totally failing.

Between these two is a narrow belt of broken veldt, with a mixed herbage, and carrying the greatest number of live stock of any part of South Africa.

The northern parts of Kaffraria, the Queenstown and Aliwal districts, Free State, Basutoland, Transvaal, and Northern Natal are densely clothed with sweet grass in the lowlands, and sour on the high mountains. Stock of all sorts thrive well, and the country is capable of carrying a heavy stock. The rainfall being good and moderately certain, cultivation without irrigation becomes practicable. But sheep are subject to more diseases than in the Karoo; and some parts, after carrying sheep for several years, give in and will not maintain them.

C

The Ostrich in its wild state was originally found over every part of South Africa; but whether it lived year in and year out in the grass veldt, or only came there occasionally when driven out of the more barren parts by exceptional droughts, is now wrapped in oblivion. That it is always looked upon as essentially a bird of the desert we know, but this may not have been from choice—not that it would not naturally prefer the soft succulent grasses of the moister parts, but that these parts were where man found the readiest means of existence, and usurped to the driving out of the Ostrich. These parts, too, teem with animal life, and consequently here were found the lion, the tiger, the wild dog and jackal, ready to prey on the Ostrich and drive him into the desert.

The Ostrich has now been introduced into every part of the Cape Colony, and appears to thrive well in all, the high grass lands subject to much cold having as yet proved the least adapted to the industry. But it will take some years' more experience to prove which parts are permanently the best. It may prove, as with the sheep, that some farms on which they throve the best the first few years eventually proved utterly unadapted to them, presumably from certain herbs essentially necessary to the health of the sheep being so sparse on the land that they were quickly destroyed.

Birds as yet are only being farmed to a small extent in the Free State, and scarcely at all in the Transvaal and Natal.

Should the birds continue healthy on the coast lands, then these will undoubtedly be the best, as from the abundant herbage and large rainfall a very much heavier stock could be kept on the same acreage as inland ; whilst the old ploughed lands would always produce succulent weeds that they are so fond of, and the farmer could grow his own grain for them ; and it may be it will prove so, as the ticks that are so detrimental to other stock can only retain a hold in three places on the Ostrich, namely, under the thighs, and on the head and upper neck—all places where the bird cannot get at them to pull them off. And the stones and alkalies in which this part is deficient can readily be supplied to them in an artificial form.

Any one who has been in Australia, or has read much of the immense scale on which wool-growing is carried on there, where a hundred thousand sheep owned and managed by one man is not uncommon, and where ten thousand is held to be the smallest number that can be profitably worked, and then compares the Cape, where ten thousand is a rarity, and a man with three thousand is looked upon as well to do, would think that the soil and climate of Australia are superior. But it is

c 2

not so. They are very similar, the difference being in favour of the Cape, which, taking it all through, will carry a heavier stock to a given area than Australia. The difference is partially caused by the farmer having to purchase his land, because at the Cape a large proportion of his capital is sunk in land; whilst in Australia, the sheep industry being mainly carried on on government ground, the squatter merely paying a grazing licence of 8d. a head per annum for the stock the land is supposed to be capable of carrying, his whole capital goes into stock. But the great cause of difference is in the labour supply. In Australia labour is dear, but it is White, and does not require close supervision; therefore, large flocks, extending to a radius of twenty miles from the homestead, are practicable; and the fewer homesteads the less expense and more profits; whilst at the Cape the labour is very cheap, but very untrustworthy, great supervision being absolutely necessary; consequently, not more than one or two out-stations are practicable, and in most cases all the sheep are kept at the homestead, where they can be counted morning and evening and guarded from thieves, without which care they would soon melt away; the greater number of homesteads, therefore, up to a certain limit, the greater profit at the Cape; and this applies equally when comparing the size of the herds of cattle and horses in Australia with the Cape herds.

The same cause works in the agricultural districts, where everything is comparatively on a small scale, and things are done in a primitive style; but this is all in favour of the young emigrant of little or no capital.

The Romans held that the sheep was shod with gold, *i.e.*, that it brought wealth wherever it went, in that it enriched the land. This is so where they are enclosed, and leave their dung on the land; but it is the very reverse where they are herded in flocks. Then they trample and loosen the best of the soil, which gets blown in heaps and washed away; whilst the under-soil gets hardened down, and the rain runs off instead of soaking in. The manure which should be re-fertilising it gets deposited in enormous heaps where the sheep are kraaled at night, and where it is utterly lost to the soil. The sheep feeding year in and year out over the same ground, the best of the herbs are eaten down and prevented from seeding, till they die out and their place is taken by inferior kinds. This is what has gone on all over the Cape Colony, till many parts have ceased to support sheep at all.

Very great injury was done to the sheep industry by over-stocking, and allowing old, sickly, and inferior sheep to breed. This was partly done in error, and partly because, previous to the discovery of diamonds, there was no market for surplus stock; but the inevit-

able result followed. The limit which Nature appears
to put to the amount of any one kind of stock on a given
area was passed, and she sent diseases and swept them
off. That this law is inevitable has been proved over
and over again in England, where game has been
attempted to be increased to an inordinate extent; but,
in spite of all care and artificial feeding, after a certain
point is reached diseases come on and sweep them off.
And so with poultry; as long as a farmer keeps a few,
what can be healthier? But let him get an excessive
number, and how quickly diseases break out and reduce
them down!

We have written thus much about the sheep, because
unless Ostrich-farmers are careful not to crowd the birds
on the land, the same results will inevitably follow with
them. The land should not be stocked to the extent
that it is at first capable of carrying. If it is, the best
herbs will be destroyed; whilst if it is only partially
stocked, in good seasons these get a chance to seed and
reproduce themselves. Even greater care is required
with the Ostrich than with the sheep, from the habit
the birds have of selecting one particular plant to feed
on, and, as long as they can get that, neglecting all
others. The only thoroughly effective way to prevent
this is to let half the farm lie idle six months, and
then the other half the next six months. The man of

means, and owning his own farm, should always have
two large camps for each troop of birds, if he would
keep an eye to the future as well as the present;
whilst the needy man on a hired farm can move to
another farm when his lease is out, and thus save
himself from the inevitable consequences of over-
stocking.

# CHAPTER IV.

## THE CAPITAL REQUIRED.

BEFORE going into this question it will be necessary to answer the question, What is capital? Most young men will exclaim, " The money my father has given me to start with;" or, "The money I have inherited, or expect to inherit." But this is a most deceptive idea of capital, as excepting in the rare cases of the young man inheriting large estates, where he has nothing to do but live off the rent-roll, or where it is so tied up that he has only to take the interest without having anything to do with managing the principal, the money inherited, unless accompanied by a thorough knowledge of the business in which it is to be employed, will soon be lost. There is an old Birmingham saying, "The man that begins business in his shirt-sleeves will end in his carriage. The man that begins in his carriage will end in his shirt-sleeves." This is the case all the world over, but doubly so in the case of a man emigrating from England to the Cape, where everything is so different.

So that we see capital in its useful sense consists

of other things besides a sum of money. The labourer's capital consists in his strong sinews and early training to manual labour. The mechanic's capital consists in .the skill he has acquired at his trade. The professional man's capital, in the money spent on his early education, and during the time of his articles or college training; it is large or small, according to his natural abilities and the use he has made of them. The merchant's capital, in a sum of money, and general knowledge of business, and business habits. The Ostrich-farmer's capital, in the money invested in his stock, and knowledge of Cape farming generally, and the management of birds; the two latter being the most important.

But what capital does the young Britisher, scion perhaps of some good family, well-educated, and sent out to a colony with perhaps no money, or with a few hundreds or a few thousands to his credit or in prospect—what capital does he possess? Much, but not yet in such a shape that he can make use of it. Before he can do that, he must acquire " colonial experience." If he is impatient, and attempts to use the money before he has acquired this, he will almost inevitably lose it; but if he has the patience to let this money be, as though he did not possess it, to let nobody know that he has it, till he has had at least two years'

thorough training in farming, mercantile pursuits, or
whatever course he has determined to adopt, he will
then find himself in a colony offering him a better
chance in the world, at the present time, than any other.

Nothing in Australia, New Zealand or Canada can
offer anything like the opening the Cape does to a young
man, with only a few hundreds of capital, to set up for
himself, if he has only had a thorough training in his
business.

All sorts of people in the towns, with a little spare
capital over and above what they require in their
business, have been investing in birds, and putting
them out on the " halves," and any young man who has
made a name for himself during his novitiate, if he can
only get helped with a few hundreds to enable him to
hire a farm and furnish himself with the necessary
plant, can get birds on the " halves." Or should the
mania for Ostrich-Farming Companies last, there will
be a brisk demand for managers and assistants.

It will be noticed that I lay far more stress on
colonial experience than on actual technical knowledge
of Ostrich-farming. It is so. The colonist born has
heard Ostriches discussed of late years both in town
and country, by man and woman, rich and poor, till
he must be dull indeed if he has not picked up a good
deal of the required knowledge—enough, at any rate,

to make a start in a small way, especially if he has had any other farm experience.

The difficulty is, how can a young man acquire this experience? To send him out to a colony without friends or relatives to go to, with the vague instructions to make his way in the world, is cruel. Occasionally such a one may tumble on his legs by great good luck, but the chances are infinitely against him. If he has capital he will be sure to invest it foolishly. We all know what " buying a pig in a poke " means; how rarely the purchaser does not find out afterwards he had better have left it alone; and yet everything the man without experience buys is a " pig in a poke."

The only chance for a man emigrating to the Cape to Ostrich-farm is to be well supplied with letters of introduction, if possible from relatives of well-to-do people living at the Cape; even then he will find it no easy matter to get on a good farm, where farming is conducted on a large scale. He must then be prepared to pay £100 premium the first year, beside being ready to buckle-to and work hard at anything — no matter what it is—to which he is set. Board and lodging he will, of course, get free, usually living in the house with the master. It is this latter that constitutes the objection farmers have to cadets, and

no wonder, with the bad household servants generally
to be had at the Cape.

But with experience once gained, then the advantages of the Cape are seen. Whilst in Australia or
New Zealand the man with less than £5,000 or
£10,000 cannot start on his own account, here a
few hundreds will give him an excellent start, with
the help of birds on the "halves." That he will have
to live close and study economy at first he must expect,
but do this, and, with ordinary luck at Ostrich-farming,
he is a made man.

# CHAPTER V.

## FENCING.

This is one of the most important subjects for the Ostrich-farmer. From the day he possesses an Ostrich, he is called upon to use his judgment as to the relative kinds best adapted to the veldt on which he is about to farm, the best suited to his means, and the labour he is able to procure. Before Ostrich-farming began, fencing in South Africa for the use of stock was an unknown thing. Farmers' horses and working cattle had to be let loose when the day's work was over; and the common excuse of a farmer, when he did not keep some appointment until a day or two after the time, was that his horses were lost, whilst half a day or a day being lost at any work through the bullocks straying was of common occurrence. But now no farmer with any enterprise would dream of farming without an enclosure for these, even if he had no birds. We have often laughed when we think of our first purchase of wire, and remember the hunt we had all over Grahamstown without finding a bundle, till we came on a merchant who had had some sent to him some years before on consignment, and which he was about shipping back as utterly unsaleable in the country ; and now look at the thousands of tons which are annually imported !

Efforts are constantly being made by the English manufacturers to send out complete ready-made fences, with iron standards and iron winding-posts ; but the standards always bend and break, while the fences are never high enough for Ostriches, and the cost is infinitely greater than a thoroughly good fence with the hard wooden posts procurable in most parts of the country. The only really good iron standard that has ever been sent out is the hollow iron post, but its cost is prohibitive ; it is never used except by government to fence some parts of the line on the railways. But " Massa Government—him very rich man."

The general fences in use consist of—

> Bush-fencing,
> Wattle-fencing,
> Post and Wire,
> The same, with Bush Interlaced,
> Stone Walls.

We will take these *seriatim.*

*Bush-fencing* consists simply of bush cut down and piled up to the height of a few feet, being either ridden on by a waggon, or, more often, put into convenient heaps, a chain slipped through the butts, and then dragged into position. This is, of course, the cheapest of all fences, but it is always decaying and constantly needing repairs; in high winds, too, it is very apt to blow over and leave gaps. But where hard bush, such as prim, baboon, &c., are plentiful, close to hand, or on a hired farm, or where the bush is so thick that there is a secondary object in view, viz., getting the bush thinned out, it makes a fairly efficient fence, and is specially well adapted for young beginners. But if used to a great extent, the time comes when, from the scarcity of labour or other reasons, it cannot be kept in repair, and the farmer soon heartily wishes he had gone in for something more expensive, but more permanent; and, if it is a fence intended to be kept up for a number of years, the constantly recurring expense of repairs will soon aggregate a larger sum than what the original cost of wire or stone wall would have been. Bush-fences made of mimosa or other soft woods will only last about six months, and are quite ineffectual for cattle.

The prime cost of bush-fencing is about sixpence a yard.

*Wattle Fences.*—These are principally used on the coast lands where the bush grows high with long

branches, and where suitable light poles can be cut
in the nearest kloof, and where, the ground being
soft, the cost of planting the poles is not much.   The
poles are planted about three feet apart, and the long
pliant boughs interlaced between them, and wattled to
the height of about 4 feet 6 inches.   It occasionally
requires a little fresh wattling on the top, when it makes
a good effective fence ; but is only durable till the
little poles rot in the ground, and should only be used
under the same circumstances as the last.   The prime
cost is about ninepence the yard.

*Wire Fencing.*—This constitutes the great bulk of
the fencing now done in the country.   We have at
present an unlimited supply of magnificent sneezewood
poles, a good sound one of which, seven inches in
diameter, will last a generation.   It has only one drawback—that birds that are unused to it, and are in
a comparatively small enclosure, are apt when they
take fright, especially at night, to run against it and
entangle their legs in the wires.   But this will never
happen if the fence is erected as we shall now advise,
though with any fence under the sun a bird may
hurt itself by the sheer force with which it comes
against it.   Where the fence is required for Ostriches
not younger than a year old, four wires are sufficient, and are better than a greater number.   Where

cattle of different sizes, or birds, are required to be enclosed or kept out, five wires are best; or for a boundary line between two neighbours even six wires may be used; or where it is required to fence sheep as well, seven wires are required. It is always preferable to use galvanised wire, not only for its greater durability, but because it shows out to the stock so much better. A wire fence for Ostriches should never be less than 4 feet 9 inches in height, as it then catches above the bend of the Ostrich's neck, and stops the bird trying to get over, as it otherwise will do. A four-wire fence should be made of all No. 3 B.W.G. wire. A five-wire fence should have the three top wires No. 3, the others No. 4. In a six or seven wire fence the lower wires may be No. 5. The number of yards of wire to the ton, the sizes measured by Birmingham wire-gauge, are :—

| No. 3 | ... | ... | 4,570 yards. |
| No. 4 | | ... | 5,455 „ |
| No. 5 | ... | ... | 6,580 „ |

But it must be borne in mind that the colonial ton is only 2,000 lbs.; so that No. 3 wire runs two yards to the pound; or, in other words, a colonial ton will do 800 yards of five wires of No. 3 wire. To construct a thoroughly good fence, the farmer should always purchase the best poles he can get, not less

D

than seven feet long, to be put two feet in the ground, and ten feet apart. Every 400 or 500 yards, or less where there are dips in the ground, the fence should break off, and the next length commence as a fresh fence, thus :—

| 400 yds. | 500 yds. | 500 yds. | 400 yds. |

This is to avoid the great strain that must otherwise come by the contraction in cold weather if carried as a continuous fence. The end poles should be eight feet long, and the heaviest poles picked out for this purpose. They should be three feet in the ground, supported by a strut in front, and tied down to the foot of a short pole put deep in the ground about ten feet behind them. This tie should be made by twice threading a wire through the top of the end pole, and through the foot of the back stay pole just mentioned, this being hove tight with a crow-bar in the same manner that the transport riders tighten their wool reims. The crow-bar can be drawn out when it is tight, as the twist will not come loose. A heavy stone should be placed, partially buried, in front of the strut, the end pole, and the back stay pole. Where the holes are in rock, the end and back stay poles should always be run in with concrete, and better still if the line poles are also. Although this may sound expensive to some farmers, I can assure them it amply repays them. The wires should never be stapled to the poles, but the poles should always be bored with a brace and auger bit. The wires are best divided as under :—

FOUR-WIRE FENCE, 4 FEET 9 INCHES HIGH.

Lower wire, 1 ft. 9 in. from ground.
Other wires, 1 ft. apart.

FIVE-WIRE FENCE, 4 FEET 9 INCHES HIGH.

Lower wire, 1 ft. 2. in. from ground.
Next two, 10 in. apart.
Next one, 11 in. „
Next one, 12 in. „

SIX-WIRE FENCE, 4 FEET 9 INCHES HIGH.

Lower wire, 8 in. from the ground.
Next two, 8 in. apart.
Next one, 10 in. „
Next one, 11 in. „
Next one, 12 in. „

SEVEN-WIRE FENCE, 4 FEET 9 INCHES HIGH.

Lower wire, 7 in. from the ground.
Next two, 6 in. apart.
Next one, 7 in. „
Next one, 8 in. „
Next one, 11 in. „
Next one, 12 in. „

At one end of each separate length of fencing either a 12 in. eye-bolt, or, best of all, one of Morton's patent

D 2

ratchets, must be put to tighten the fencing should
it at any time get slack, as it is everything with a wire
fence to keep it as tight as a drum. The wire is hove
up at the other end by a piece of wood with two cross-
pieces of wood let in it, and used as a windlass. An old
yoke with a hole bored through the centre of it does
very well for this purpose; the wire when tight being
caught by an implement called an elbow whilst it is
being taken off the windlass, and made fast round the
post. If you have not an elbow the hole must be
plugged, but this is always apt to slip and give trouble.
One perpendicular tie of No. 5 wire connecting the
wires should be put between each two posts.

Care should be taken that the men do not simply
take hold of an end of wire in the coil and walk away
with it. The wire should be carefully uncoiled, not a
turn being allowed to slip, as otherwise the wire will be
weakened, and it will never come properly straight and
stiff. Most workmen now understand how to join the
wires. It is done by overlapping the two ends and
nipping them with a screw-hammer, or with implements
sold for the purpose, then twisting each end with short
turns round the opposite wire with an iron with a hole
in the end. Where the post-holes are in hard rock they
can be cut out with a chisel-pointed steel jumper and
hammer.

The cost of a mile of 5 wire fence as here described will be

|  | £ | s. | d. |
|---|---|---|---|
| 4,900 lbs. at 22s. 6d. | 55 | 2 | 6 |
| 546 posts at 1s. 3d. | 34 | 2 | 6 |
| 20 Morton's ratchets at 4s. | 4 | 0 | 0 |
| Labour at 1s. 3d. a post | 34 | 2 | 6 |
| 4 casks of cement at 30s. | 6 | 0 | 0 |
| Wear and tear of tools | 3 | 0 | 0 |
| Moving material | 3 | 0 | 0 |
|  | £139 | 7 | 6 |

or 1s. 7d. per yard. This appears expensive, but when put up it is a perfect fence, and should scarcely require touching for years, as a broken wire is a very rare sight. Like every other good thing, it must be paid for. When erected in ground the cost of the cement would be saved. The prices I have given are the current prices in Grahamstown at the present time. Further up country the cost of carriage of the material must be added; whilst it must be borne in mind that labourers require tents or other accommodation, which often adds to the expense.

It will be noted that the weight of wire given includes the ties, and the number of posts includes what is necessary for breaking it into lengths as before described. A 6 or 7 wire fence does not cost much more, as then lighter wires are used, and labourers generally take the work at so much the post, irrespective of the number of wires. But for Ostriches, the greater the number of wires above five the greater are the chances of their entangling themselves.

*Post and Wire with Bush interlaced.*—A fair fence costing less than the last is sometimes made by putting the posts fifteen feet apart, with only three wires, and these put up roughly and slack, with bush interlaced. Of course this is nothing like the permanent fence that the last is, but it is the cheapest thing that a man out on the Karoo flats, where bush is scarce, can put up, and is often used by men who, not understanding how to put up a wire fence properly, think their birds will come to grief unless they have the interlacing bush.

*Stone Walls.*—The great advantage of a stone wall over other dead fences is, that whilst being permanent it serves for small as well as large stock, and at the same time makes a considerable break-wind; and on a sandstone formation, where stone of a good square shape can be procured near the site of the proposed fence, it is the best. The drawbacks to it are the time it takes to complete any considerable length of fencing; and consequently those who want an immediate return from their capital cannot afford it, as the money laid out on the fencing, until the enclosure is completed, earns nothing. It is also always liable to fall into gaps, and is useless for goats, who jump over it. Where the stone is of a shaly nature it is useless for dry stone walls, as in a few years the stone will crumble away ; and where it is of a round bouldery nature it requires a very experienced man to pack it so that it will not fall.

A wall should be four feet high, three feet at the base, and eighteen inches at the top, but if the stone is very good, the base need not be so wide as this. The great thing to look out for is that the men do not put in "shiners"—that is, stones showing their longest face to the front. They should put a great number of "through" stones—that is, stones going right through from one side to the other, and the stones on the two sides of the wall should constantly overlap from one side to the other. If this is not done, although the wall may stand all right for a year or two, it will then begin to fall into gaps in all directions. The usual price for quarrying the stone and packing the wall is 1s. 6d. per yard, and this usually includes the men loading the stone on and off the wagon, the farmer finding wagon and oxen, also leader and driver, who assist with the loading and off-loading. The wear and tear to wagon and oxen is great, and if the stone has to be ridden any considerable distance it will put another shilling a yard on the cost of the wall.

Although, as a rule, stone walling may be con-

sidered as safe for birds as any other fence, I have
known it, when built with stone from an igneous formation, to be the cause of many birds injuring themselves
by kicking against the sharp points when fighting with
each other on opposite sides of a wall, and I have also
known serious losses to occur where birds have stam-
peded at night, and have run with great force against it,
many killing themselves.

For fencing in lands and gardens it beats anything,
as it keeps out porcupines and hares, which are often
so destructive, especially in the sweet veldt.

For little short lengths of fencing, where bush is
not procurable, old tire-irons off the hind-wheels of
wagons, when straightened and bolted on to sneezewood
posts, make a very strong and durable fence. These
can be bought from the wagon-makers for 5s. each,
ready bored for three bolts; but the fence becomes too
expensive except in special cases. And the same thing
applies to imported fences of bar-iron and standards,
which come very expensive if high enough for Ostriches.

Live fences have been very little used in the colony.
The easiest grown are the American aloe and the
prickly pear, but the former is liable to be destroyed
by moles whilst the plants are young, and the latter
is a nuisance to the birds when the fruit is ripe. Pome-
granate, quince, and other things are often used where

they can be irrigated and the soil is moist, but of course
this is only the case in lands or gardens.

*Mutual Fencing.*—By this we mean a boundary
fence erected between two neighbours, each sharing
the expense. All the Australasian colonies have found
it necessary to legislate on this matter, to save the
enterprising farmers from being deterred from fencing
in their land, by the very natural feeling of not caring
to bear the whole expense of erecting a fence which
will benefit the adjoining neighbour equally with themselves ; whilst anything that tends to deter a man
from fencing in his land is not only detrimental to the
individual but to the whole community. And as it is
of primary importance, both to the state and to everybody in the country, that the land should be made
to produce as much as possible, and as it is an
undisputed fact that enclosed land will carry a much
heavier stock than unenclosed land where the stock
is herded, these countries have seen it is one of
those subjects in which private rights and inclinations
must be made to give way to the general weal. And
seeing that the country is saved from being deteriorated
when it is enclosed, whereas it rapidly deteriorates
when the stock is driven about in flocks, they have
all passed acts varying in detail, but all embracing
the main feature, that where a farmer fences a boun-

dary line, the neighbour should be compelled to con-
tribute half the cost.

Some years ago a movement was made in the colony
to get legislation on this subject, but great opposition was
shown to it by the less enterprising part of the community, and no act has succeeded in passing. Whilst
we should hesitate to go the length of the Australians
in compelling an unwilling neighbour to find half the
necessary capital, which, if his financial position was
bad, might prove ruinous, much of this difficulty would
have been met by allowing the man that wants to
fence to find all the capital, and then to take a pre-
ferential lien on the other man's farm to the amount
of 10 per cent. annually on the half-cost of the fence
for fourteen years, by which time, if we reckon the
normal rate of interest on money at 6 per cent., the
extra 4 per cent. would have formed a sinking fund,
which in fourteen years would have extinguished
the debt. And as the property would have been improved to a greater extent than the half cost of the
fence, the mortgagees would not be affected by this lien
being preferent. Or, better still, if the government
were to advance the money on these terms, as it now
does on irrigation works, which are much more liable
to destruction, and probably of less advantage to the
country than fencing.

It is often urged that the fencing of a particular boundary line may be of more advantage to one farm than another : it often is so, but any hardship on this score could be met by the unwilling party having the right to call in arbitrators to decide on the relative portions of expense each farm should bear.

Another suggestion which has been made, is that the unwilling man should not be called upon for his half the expense unless he used the fence as part of an enclosure, or made some other fence abutting on to it. It would have been wise if this scheme had been accepted, as then the most sensitive could not have feared that there would be any oppression towards the poorer or unwilling man. As it is, whole tracts of country lie unfenced and producing little or nothing towards the general wealth of the country, which would otherwise have been fenced and have become highly productive.

It is found in practice that neighbours seldom agree as to erecting a mutual boundary fence ; in consequence the fencing man is driven to fence a few yards inside his boundary, with the object of compelling his neighbour to share the expense before he can make use of the fence. This, if it continues, will, in the course of time, bring endless disputes as to where the boundaries of the farms are.

Where the cost of the fence is to be mutually

borne, the one that undertakes to erect the fence should be very careful to have the following points settled before he does so :—*First,* that the boundary stones as standing shall be admitted as correct; this is highly essential, as in a long boundary line some of the stones are sure not to be in line, and after the fence is erected the other man might refuse payment on the grounds that the fence was not where it ought to be. We knew a case in point, where, after the fence was erected, the man not only refused payment, but by a law-suit compelled his neighbour to take up the fence on the grounds that it was a few feet out, and to again erect it in terms of his contract. *Second,* the nature and quality of the fence should be clearly defined, and it should also be stated that the one half is to stand immediately on one side of the beacon stones, and the other half on the opposite side, each party being bound to keep in repair the part that stands on his own land. *Third,* it should be stated in the contract that any slight unintentional divergence from the true line shall not be disputed, and that as long as the spirit of the contract has been fairly acted up to there shall be no dispute. Unless these points are conceded, a man had much better fence inside his boundary at his own cost.

# CHAPTER VI.

## THE PROFITS FROM OSTRICHES.

WHAT return do birds give on the capital invested? This would be the first question asked by any one thinking of going in for farming. It is a question very few even of those that have been at it some years could answer, and of which the public have the most wild ideas, or else the promoters of the joint-stock companies that have been lately started in all directions would never have the barefacedness to advertise prospectuses promising the public from 40 to 100 per cent. per annum on their investment; including in this even the capital sunk in land, buildings, dams, &c. &c., which give no direct return, and which in England would represent the landlord's investment, and which is subject to scarcely any risk, the fencing, buildings, wagons, &c., being the only part subject to natural decay. A return on the whole of this part of the capital of 15 per cent. per annum would be a good return.

Now where the private individual or company combine both ownership and occupation, it may be taken that the dead capital, *i.e.*, that which will give no direct return, is a half of the total investment under indifferent management, or where the buildings, &c., are of a solid, permanent kind, and the future is looked to as well as the present; or a third, where the screw is put on, and the improvements are not of such a permanent character.

No doubt this statement will make many farmers who are not in the habit of keeping books, and looking carefully into things, exclaim "Nothing of the sort." To such I say, sit down, price and total up the cost of everything employed, and you will be astonished.

At any rate, taking the prospectus now before me of a company lately successfully floated in Grahamstown, and for which hundreds of shares were applied for more than were available, and in which the promoters promised a net return of over 40 per cent. the first year, and over 100 per cent. in subsequent years, the investment was :—

| | |
|---|---:|
| Farm with buildings, fencing, &c., &c. ... | £4,225 |
| Birds and eggs ... ... ... ... ... ... | 5,775 |
| Available for other purposes ... ... ... | 2,000 |
| | 12,000 |

The "available for other purposes" would mean transfer dues, wagons, oxen, horses, carts, implements, current expenses, &c. So that more than one-half was

here calculated as dead capital; consequently the birds
were represented to pay, over and above expenses of
management and feeding, 185 per cent. per annum.

Of course the thing is absurd; did birds pay anything like this, we should have had ere this every
shopkeeper selling off his stock, hiring strips of land,
and putting every penny he could get hold of into birds.
That some pairs of birds will have four nests in a season,
and bring out, say, twelve chicks in each nest, which
might be sold for £6 each at a day old, we all know.
And that this may be greatly increased by artificial
hatching we know, as see the almost fabulous returns I
made by this means, as given in the chapter on Artificial Hatching, where you will see that one set of birds
gave a gross return of £1,676 in one year. But that
this is any criterion of what a general stock can be
trusted to do, we deny.

We know an estate where all the land has not been
stocked, and where everything is done with a liberal
hand, and in the most permanent style, which has
averaged for the last six years a net return of 30 per
cent. per annum on the total investment, including cost
of land and all improvements. As also one which, for
the four years 1872, 1873, 1874 and 1875, averaged a
net return on the capital invested of 66½ per cent. per
annum; but in this latter case the land was hired,

everything was studied to lessen the amount of the dead capital, and the expenses were pared down to the lowest possible shilling, whilst the farmer worked terribly hard with both hands and head, and thoroughly understood his business.

But this was before "fever" in the chicks was known, and when ostriches altogether were healthier, and kept their condition with less feeding. Even then the returns varied exceedingly: thus, whilst in 1872 the net profits were considerably over 100 per cent., in 1873 and 1874 they were under 50 per cent.

One of the best items of profit to a farmer is the increased value of his troop of plucking birds. Thus a bird twelve months old, value say £22, would be at four years old worth £50, besides having given on an average £12 a year in feathers; so that, allowing a loss of 10 per cent. per annum in deaths, the return is grand.

Each bird should give one pound weight of feathers, if plucked as advised in the chapter on Plucking. There should be fifty quill feathers: this includes, say, four fancy-coloured in each wing. The tails vary exceedingly in the number of feathers—from 75 to 100. A good average all round is, say, quills, 5 ounces; tail, 5 ounces; blacks or drabs, 6 ounces.

# CHAPTER VII.

## BIRDS ON THE HALVES.

THE system of farming birds on the halves is now so general, that the leading features of it are familiar to most people at the Cape, but in detail agreements vary much; many even take them without any written agreement, but this is a most objectionable practice. We now give examples of fair agreements at the present time, in both the cases of breeding birds and plucking birds.

### BREEDING BIRDS.

Agreement made and entered into between Mr. A., on the first part, and Mr. B., on the second part, by which—

1. The first-named agrees to lend the second-named two pairs of guaranteed breeding Ostriches, to be farmed by the second-named on the halves. That is, Mr. B. is to find grazing, and to bear all and every expense connected with the birds.

2. The birds to remain, as now, the sole property of Mr. A.

3. The proceeds of all sale of feathers to be equally divided by Mr. B. within one month of each sale, and original account sales submitted by him to Mr. A.

4. Any chicks from these birds to be sold by Mr. B. between the ages of three and six months, but only at such price as Mr. A. shall consent to. If not sold when six months old, then to be

E

sold by public auction in the Y——a public market, to which place he shall bring them, and the proceeds equally divided.

5. In the event of the death or loss of any of these birds, Mr. B. shall pay to Mr. A., within two months of such death or loss, the half value of the same, the value of a cock bird being agreed to be £   , the value of a hen bird £   .

6. On or about the first day of each calendar month, Mr. B. shall send to Mr. A. a report in writing of the state of his venture, answering therein any reasonable questions Mr. A. may have submitted to him.

7. Any breach of this contract to be held good and sufficient grounds for the aggrieved party to cancel the same, without notice, irrespective of any other remedy he may seek.

8. This agreement to cease on six months' notice being given on either side.

9. In any place where Mr. A. is here named, it shall be taken to mean himself or his duly appointed substitute.

Done at                    this      day of            18   .

Witnesses to ⎰ C.                    Signed ⎰ A.
Signatures  ⎱ D.                            ⎱ B.

These agreements are often for a term of years, and B. no doubt would prefer this; but A. often finds he has been mistaken in his man, that the birds are doing badly, and his investment is a bad one, when he will be very glad to avail himself of the six months' notice we have above provided for.   On the other hand, if B. makes them do well, he may be sure A. will be only too glad to leave them with him.

We will now consider an agreement for, let us say, fifty birds, one year old.   This is a matter requiring more consideration. We have known some cases of a man signing an agreement rashly, and afterwards finding that he was liable to replace, out of the feather money, any deaths, not by birds of the same age as those he took over, but by birds of the same age as those that died; whilst he was getting no interest on the increased value of the remainder: so that since the birds would give about the same feather return the first year as the last, any death the first year would only take about £20 of the feather money to make good; whilst the last year, since he would have to make good a four-year-old bird, it would take £50. So that, although he might do well the first two years, if he had many deaths the last two he would be ruined. In fact, if he had only ordinary luck with them, he would find at the end of his term he had cleared nothing.

But we do not advise either party to have anything to do with replacing the birds that die. Let them be paid for, as they die, out of the feather money; and when a number are dead, it is open for them to make a fresh agreement for another lot. This keeps the transaction simple, whilst the other will be found in practice to open the flood-gates to trickery and misunderstanding. We here give an agreement on this plan :—

E 2

Agreement made and entered into between Mr. A., on the first part, and Mr. B., on the second part, by which—

1. The first-named agrees to lend the second-named fifty ostriches, averaging in age one year, to be farmed by the second-named on the halves—that is, Mr. B. is to find grazing and to bear all and every expense connected with the birds.

2. The birds to remain, as now, the sole property of Mr. A.

3. The value of these birds is agreed between the above-named parties to be twenty pounds sterling each.

4. That the proceeds of all feathers sold from these birds shall be equally divided by Mr. B. within one month of such sale, who shall submit to Mr. A. original account sales of such feathers: provided that, before any such division of money, Mr. B. shall pay out of it to Mr. A. the sum of £20 for every bird that has died or been lost up to that date; and if such feather money is not sufficient to pay for all so deficient, the remainder shall be made up out of the next feather sales.

5. That a bird shall be deemed lost after it has been missing one calendar month; but should it afterwards be recovered, Mr. A. shall refund to Mr. B. £10 sterling for such bird.

6. On or about the first day of each calendar month Mr. B. shall send to Mr. A. a report in writing of the state of his venture, answering therein any reasonable questions Mr. A. may have submitted to him.

7. This agreement to terminate three years from the date thereof. At its expiration Mr. B. shall deliver the birds to Mr. A. in Y——n, to be sold by him at auction on the public market, who shall pay to Mr. B. one-third of whatever they may net over and above £20 each.

8. Any breach of this contract to be held good and sufficient grounds for the aggrieved party to cancel the same, irrespective of any other remedy he may seek.

9. In any place where Mr. A. is here named, it shall be taken to mean himself or his duly-appointed substitute.

10. In the event of any deaths or losses of the birds after the last sale of feathers, or any deficiency at the last sale to meet former losses, Mr. B. shall pay to Mr. A. the sum of £10 sterling for such bird so deficient.

11. The feathers not to be taken oftener than once in eight months.

Done at                    this          day of                    18      .

Witnesses to { C.                         Signed { A.
Signatures   { D.                                 { B.

We have here supposed that the farmer is to get a share in the increased value of the birds when sold; we know that this is not general, but we do not see that he has a fair chance of benefiting himself unless he gets this, at any rate not in proportion to the risk he runs.

Allowing for those that die having given no feathers, or only a few, we cannot safely reckon on more than £12 a head return all round, which would give £600: but taking 10 per cent. to be a fair average for deaths and losses, this will take off £100, leaving £250 each for the year's return, but out of his share the farmer will have to pay all expenses.

But supposing present prices to be maintained, at the end of the three years the birds would be worth £50 each. Now, allowing 10 per cent. per annum for deaths, there would be thirty-seven birds to sell, which would give £1,111 more than the original cost; and if the farmer got a third, he would have £370 to receive. It would then have paid him handsomely.

# CHAPTER VIII.

## FARMING PARTNERSHIPS.

WE do not advise any one to try starting on his own account with less stock than we have given in our last chapter. If he has not the capital and cannot get birds on the halves, his only other resource is to take a partner. If he can get a sleeping partner who is willing to put in, say, £2,000 against his £500 and services as manager, he is infinitely better off than if he took birds on the halves, because he will then have to give up only half the net earnings, in the place of half the gross earnings if the birds are on the halves; and yet it may answer the sleeping partner quite as well, as he then has a voice in the management, and his birds will not suffer for want of liberal treatment, as is so often the case where an impecunious man has the birds on the halves.

Even if he cannot get one man to put in £2,000, he may get four men to put in £500 each, when each of these will get an eighth of the net earnings. This to a certain extent constitutes a company, but with the great pull in their favour that the managing partner, having the greatest interest of any of them in the success of the concern, will require no supervision; all that the sleeping partners need do is to look into the books and see that they get their due portion. There are no brokers' fees, no outlay on huge advertisements of the prospectus, no promotion money, no secretary to pay, and no directors' fees, and, above all, no swindling by shareholders and directors slipping in stock or stores at an outrageous price.

It is partnerships like this that have proved so pre-eminently successful in wool-growing in Australia.

Another kind of partnership which is likely to become much more general is :—A. owns a suitable farm, which he gives rent-free for the use of a partnership between himself and B., as a set-off against B.'s services as manager, each putting in half the working capital; but B. has only £500, and the half-capital would be £1,250. A. therefore agrees to advance the £750 B. is short of, taking his bills at one, two, and three years, bearing interest at 6 per cent. per annum. We have personally known this kind of partnership to work with the greatest success. B. thoroughly understands his business, or else A. would have had nothing to do with him; therefore the more A. leaves him alone the better. But this just suits A., who has got his own business to attend to. A. should, however, guard himself by registering the concern under the Limited Liability Act, and should provide in the partnership deed that no joint promissory note shall be given, or mutual debt incurred, and no stock bought or sold, except by joint consent.

A. being the owner of the land can consent to take over from the partnership, at its expiration, any improvements at one-half their value. By this means he enables B. to provide the birds with proper accommodation, whilst he guards against B. being extravagant by the quarter loss he would sustain. It also gives B. an incentive to stick to the partnership for its full period, by the loss of all claim to compensation for improvements that its termination earlier would entail. A. should further guard himself by stipulating that any infringement of the deed, *ipso facto*, constitutes full grounds for the aggrieved party to break up the partnership if he thinks fit, irrespective of any other remedy he may seek. The deed should also state that B. is to reside on the farm, and give his whole and undivided attention to managing it, agreeing not to engage in any other occupation ; also that B.'s household expenses are to be borne by himself. In fact, it should be as precise as possible, leaving no loopholes for future misunderstanding.

But another, and apparently the simplest kind of partnership, namely, that where two men put their money together and jointly farm on the same farm, we cannot advise, except where they are brothers, or are as brothers. With mercantile or professional men the thing is feasible, and of course is daily done, but then they do not have to live in the same house, they only meet at the office, when each has his own department, and clashing is thus avoided. All they need is to be agreed as to the general manner in which their business shall be conducted, and then to use mutual forbearance in carrying it out. But in farming it is impossible to avoid almost hourly clashing; and besides this, they will be living together, which greatly increases the chances of disagreement.

Man and wife often find it difficult to rub along smoothly, with their two spheres of labour so utterly distinct; and two men living in the same house, and farming together, are in nearly as close union, with all the favourable circumstances of agreement removed. If one is older, and has more experience than the other, and the younger agrees in the deed to let the voice of the senior be final in all matters, it may work; without this, you might as well put two captains in command of one ship and think they would agree.

# CHAPTER IX.

## TRAVELLING WITH BIRDS.

YOUNG beginners often meet with great trouble, and sometimes serious loss, in removing their birds, after purchasing, from a want of knowledge of how to manage them.

At all times, with the most experienced men, removing birds where they have been long in camps and have become unused to strange sights and sounds, is a matter of anxiety, forethought and patience, especially the first two days' journey, though after that time the birds get accustomed to it, and there is little difficulty, unless dogs are met with and chase them.

With birds of all ages, a man should walk in front with a bag of mealies, dropping a few as he goes along, and calling to the birds, the other men driving on behind being armed with light thorn-bushes, which are infinitely superior to whips, as, if the birds take fright and try to turn back, the thorn-bushes turn them where whips are useless; besides, whips spoil the plumage and are apt to catch in the birds' legs and throw them down, especially when the whips get wet.

With chicks and troops of plucking birds there is little difficulty ; the main danger is at night, when, if put into a strange kraal or enclosure they are apt to take a panic and rush against a fence, injuring themselves. If the journey is for more than two days the traveller should have a wagon or cart, carrying grain and going in front; they then become attached to it, and by turning out of the road at night and camping, the birds will lie quietly round and the risks of strange kraals are avoided.

Birds stand travelling very well, and will keep up their 25 to 30 miles a day without feeling it ; but they should not be taken out of a walk, and should be liberally fed with grain, say three or four pounds a day each. If the journey is short, and time is pressing, they can be taken from 40 to 50 miles a day, when they can be taken at a good swing for miles at a stretch down-hill or on level ground, but if pushed whilst going up-hill they soon knock up and become dangerously distressed.

Persons should be very careful of trying to remove birds that have been long in a garden or small enclosure where they do not see other stock, or wild bucks ; such birds when taken out will sometimes take a terrible panic, and run till they drop down dead or paralysed. Such a case happened last year in Grahams-

town, where a man tried to remove 18 birds that had
been reared and kept in a small yard. I had been
consulted by one of the parties about it, and had told
them that the thing was impossible without first getting
them into a strong paddock and letting them for a
month or two get thoroughly accustomed to strange
sights ; it was, however, attempted without, when what
I predicted happened : the birds at once bolted in every
direction, and only six were ever recovered that lived
afterwards ; some ran till they dropped dead, others
killed themselves against fences, and others dropped
down, and although they lived for days never stood
up again.

Breeding birds are the worst to remove, from having
been in their small camps ; they are always rather
timid, and, where more than one pair has to be removed
at a time the difficulty is increased by their fighting.
If there is a camp round the homestead, or even a
good kraal, they should be brought there in pairs, and
then, all being more or less timid at the strange place,
they will not be nearly so likely to fight seriously. By
keeping them there for twenty-four hours and working
with them, much time is often saved, and the birds
do not throw themselves back in breeding, as they
invariably do if they get raced about much in moving.
To move a pair of breeding birds that have been long

camped off, at least four men should be employed, all armed with bushes, and one of them at least mounted.

Sometimes a bird will become frightened at a gateway, and will not pass it ; it should then be caught by the neck by one man, another man on each side seizing it and pushing it along, when it can be taken anywhere.

Hobbling and all other like practices are quite unnecessary, and constantly result in the serious injury or death of the bird. The great secret is to take things quietly, and never to gallop after a bird ; when he " scricks " and runs away, if you can cut him off and turn him, well and good ; but novices often gallop after a bird, when the harder they gallop the harder the bird goes and the greater fright he gets ; whereas, if they had got off their horses and lit their pipes first, they would generally have found the bird had only gone a short distance, and was waiting for them.

Much harm is often done by impatience. Constantly at first a bird will not come through the gate of its enclosure, and force is used, instead of coaxing ; the bird is thus frightened, and gives much trouble.

# CHAPTER X.

WE will suppose a young man, a bachelor, has gone through his novitiate on some farm, has cut his wisdom teeth, and has £2,500 to invest. How had this capital be best invested?

We will suppose he has decided to try up-country and not on the coast, the capabilities of which for birds have yet to be proved; but should it prove that the birds will remain in health on the coast, a much smaller farm than is given below would be sufficient.

A farm of, say, 3,000 to 4,000 acres of suitable land, with good permanent water, with some sort of a house and a couple of outbuildings, has been leased for five years at, say, a rental of £150 a year. It has probably been used for cattle, there is a kraal, there is plenty of bush near the homestead and in other parts, but there are no camps.

The first thing is to buy a cart and six oxen, a few simple articles of furniture and cooking utensils, a couple of horses, a dozen cows and a bull, fifty head of poultry, provisions and rations for four or five men, axes, and a few carpentering tools, &c.; with these our friend tracks on to the farm. His first difficulty will be to get men, but having succeeded in this, he sets to and makes a bush enclosure, say 300 yards square.

He should then purchase, say, fifty young birds a year old; these he will have herded by day, and put in his enclosure at night. His next step will be to commence, say, a line of six breeding camps—of course, if possible, taking advantage of anything in the shape of a natural fence—these should be not less than 300 yards square; as he completes them he can purchase, say, four pairs of thoroughly good breeding birds, and two pairs of three or four year olds. He should now purchase an incubator, not necessarily large, but the best kind he can get ; as, even if he does not mean to incubate as a regular thing, every farmer should have one as a stand-by, in case of accidents. If he has a neighbour with a family, he will probably be able to get his supply of meat from him.

Our friend will now be started, and his capital will be invested somewhat as under :—

| | |
|---|---:|
| Cart and gear ... ... ... ... ... ... | £40 |
| 6 Oxen ... ... ... ... ... ... | 60 |
| 12 Cows ... ... ... ... ... ... | 144 |
| 1 Bull ... ... ... ... ... ... ... | 10 |
| Poultry ... ... ... ... ... ... | 6 |
| Furniture, gun, tools, provisions, servants' rations, plough, &c. ... ... ... ... ... | 120 |

| | | | | |
|---|---|---|---|---|
| 2 Horses, saddles, and bridles | ... | ... | ... | 40 |
| 1 Incubator ... | .. | ... | ... | 40 |
| Cash in hand for wages and petty | | ... | ... | 40 |
| | | | | 500 |
| 50 Young birds ... | ... | ... | ... | 1,000 |
| 4 Pairs good guaranteed breeders | | ... | ... | 800 |
| 2 Pairs 3½-year-old birds ... | ... | ... | ... | 200 |
| | | | Total | 2,500 |

It will be seen here that the capital over and above that invested in the birds is a fifth of the total; but if he was on veldt, where the bush is scarce, he would have to go in, at any rate partially, for wire, which would bring this item up to a quarter of the whole, and correspondingly reduce his returns. There will be considerable saving of labour after the wire is once up, but this will probably be counterbalanced by the greater liability to accidents with wire.

What shall we say as to the returns our friend may expect? This we have partially answered in another chapter, where we have given the case of a man under somewhat similar circumstances, who made in one year a net profit of over a hundred per cent., and over a considerable number of years made an average of 66½ per cent.; and in his case he had scarcely any bush, and was compelled to use wire. But he worked with both hands and brain in a manner few would be found

THE OSTRICH (STRUTHIO CAMELUS).

to do; and honesty compels us to say that, owing to the greater prevalence of disease in birds, and other causes, we doubt whether the same man under the same circumstances could do it now.

But let us suppose the commoner case of a young man who has only got £500 to invest, but is promised birds on the halves. We should then advise him to invest his capital as in the first £500 in the former case, and to get on the halves a proportion of breeding and feather birds as there described. Breeding birds, where they succeed, undoubtedly pay infinitely the best; but the risk is correspondingly greater, and every man should have a moderate troop of plucking birds to meet the rent and expenses in case of a bad season with the breeders. Of course, with birds on the halves our young friend has got a tough up-hill game to fight, but "Faint heart never won fair lady," or a fortune.

As soon as our friend has got his birds comfortably located on his farm, he should commence a camp of say 1,000 acres in which to put his plucking birds, and so have them to a considerable extent off his hands by the time his first chicks come.

A farm of the size we have named is more veldt than he will require at first, but he must have room for future increase, and nothing will damage his chance

F

of success more than being cramped up. If the sight of part of it lying idle grieves him, he could take oxen on to graze.

If possible, let him select a farm that has on it especially plenty of spec boom and carl prickly pear. Without these, the first severe drought that comes, if mealies are scarce, will play havoc with his farming.

# CHAPTER XI.

## MANAGING A TROOP OF PLUCKING BIRDS.

OSTRICHES are generally designated as chicks up to seven or eight months old, or as long as they have still got their first crop of feathers on. From then till a year old, they are called young birds. From one to four years old, they are called plucking or feather birds. The next two years they are properly designated as four and five year old birds; but in advertisements of sales and prospectuses of companies they are often called breeding birds, but this is only a trick to swell the appearance of the thing. We have heard of cases of men buying birds as breeding birds, thinking they were buying birds that had already bred, and finding afterwards that they were only four or five year old birds that had not yet bred, and were consequently only worth about half what they gave. Birds that have been paired off in separate camps, but have not yet bred, are often called "camped-off birds." As they may be camped off at any age, the term conveys very little information, though four years old is the usual age for camping them off. After they have bred they

F 2

become "guaranteed breeders," and have changed their designation for the last time.

The distinguishing marks of the different ages are somewhat as follows, though it must be borne in mind that a very forward bird of one age will have many of the marks of the age above him, whilst a backward bird will have many of the marks of the age below.

*Six-and-a-half months old.*—The quill feathers will be ready to cut; some of the body feathers will have begun to change; some of the cocks will show yellow in the front of the legs.

*Twelve months old.*—The second growth of quill feathers should be showing; some of the cocks should begin to show black feathers; all cocks should show white on legs and bill.

*Two years old.*—All the chicken feathers should have gone from the back, and the cocks should show quite black, or nearly so. Most of the little white belly feathers should have been replaced by blacks or drabs, according to sex.

*Three years old.*—There should not be a single chicken feather to be found on the body; the last place from which they disappear is where the neck joins the body. Every vestige of the white belly feathers has gone. The bird's plumage has reached perfection; some of the cocks will be red in front of the leg and on the bill.

*Four years old.*—The birds have reached maturity. The breeding organs are fully developed; the cocks in season will have the back sinews of the leg pink, the front of the leg and the bill scarlet, and much of the fineness of the feet, the leg, and the lines of the body will have gone.

*Five years old and upwards.*—The only distinguishing marks we know are a generally coarser look of the limbs and body, and an increased coarseness of the scaling in front of the legs and feet.

Up to twelve months old the birds should be treated as chicks, being herded and fed with one pound each of either wheat, barley, or Kaffir corn, shedded in wet weather, and green food cut up for them when the veldt is dry. After this age they can be put in a large camp, of not less than ten acres to a bird, of ordinary South African veldt, and left to shift for themselves; but an opportunity should be selected for doing this when the veldt is in prime order, and even then they will be very apt to take to hanging up and down the fence nearest the homestead, and will require to be partially herded for a time in the camp.

For the next two years they will require watching, and, if the veldt should get dry, to be fed; each year as they get older they will get more robust, and better able to stand hardship and scarcity of food. Up to three years old they often suffer terribly from internal parasites, and occasionally, especially if food is scarce, require to be physicked (*see* DISEASES, &c.). If your fences are good, once a fortnight is quite often enough to muster them.

Every farmer should keep a stock book, and carefully note the count in each camp. Trusting to memory is uncertain; a bird is taken out for some reason, or some are sold, or one dies, and these are very apt to be forgotten, and much trouble and uncertainty as to what the count should be is thus caused.

The days of cutting the feathers or pulling the stumps of every bird on the farm should be carefully noted in a book. If this is not done the feathers will be very apt to be left a few days too long, and be considerably damaged; or else, perhaps, in a very busy season, much time will be lost by getting the birds up to pluck, and then finding that the feathers are not ready.

### BRANDING.

Every bird should be branded with the owner's initials in large letters of about four inches. The branding-iron should not be more than an eighth of an inch broad on the burning edge. If many birds are to be branded there should be three irons, to ensure their being red-hot. The birds should be put in the plucking-box, and a few mealies thrown to them to attract their attention from the operator, when no holding will be required. The irons being red-hot, they only require to be applied and removed almost instantaneously, and then a dab of oil should be put on the place. The mistake that is generally made is keeping the iron on too long, thus destroying the skin and making a sore. On a large establishment there should be an age-brand as well. Pieces of fencing-wire twisted into any required shape make the best branding-irons that can be used for either age or quality branding.

Every plucking time, any extra well-feathered bird should receive a private brand, and every particularly inferior one another. This can also be done by notching the toes with a file; but these will grow out in time.

Birds can be branded when a few months old, but the skin is then very thin, and the operation must be done with care.

When the birds are three years old, some of the hens will endeavour to get out of the camp and go off, generally in a northerly direction; and it is astonishing what places they will get through at this time, though up to this period if bred on the farm a very moderate fence will have sufficed. But where up-country birds are brought coast-wise, for months they will try their utmost to get away northwards—sticking to the north fence of their camp, starving and fretting, and at last compelling the farmer to herd them in their camp.

In the fearful droughts to which every part of South Africa is more or less subject, there will occasionally come a time when on the very best of veldt there is little for the birds to eat, when even the spec boom shrivels and seems to lose its sustaining power as food; under these circumstances grain alone will not keep the birds in a healthy condition. And it is in these times that the farmer with plenty of carl prickly pear reaps the advantage, as he can then bring the plucking birds into smaller camps, and either with large butchers' knives, or with the machines known as Ostrich food-cutters, and which are made for the purpose, cut up once a day as much of it as they can eat. This, with a pound of grain each daily, will keep them in good trim.

The prickly pear, especially the thorny kind, is a great nuisance in the summer when the fruit is ripe, as, if other food is scarce, the birds will go for the fruit and get the little thorns in their eyes, sometimes almost blinding themselves for a time; but, if left alone, in a few days they recover, but often not before they have become terribly thin.

The plucking birds should have access to water, and be well supplied with crushed bones; if a few heaps of these are thrown out in their camp, they will find them when they require the phosphates the bones contain.

On the coast, or places where mangel-wurzel can be cultivated, it makes an excellent food for birds; and where there is no prickly pear, something of the sort should always be cultivated, in case of drought or locusts coming.

For the benefit of my English readers, I should explain that "mealies" is the Cape name for maize or Indian corn.

# CHAPTER XII.

In the first days of Ostrich-farming the feathers were plucked every six months, the feathers in that length of time, almost to a day, having apparently attained their full growth, but varying a little according to the condition the bird was in. I say apparently, because, although the fluffy part of the feather is at its longest, and the blood-vein in the feather will have dried as far down as the junction of the feather with the wing, yet the stalk below the skin is still alive and growing. It was soon found that this constant pulling before the feather was ripe caused it in each successive growth to become shorter, and the quill stiffer, till by the time the bird was five or six years old the feathers were of little value. But the feathers cannot be left after the blood-vessel has dried up as far down as the junction of the wing, as the vitality of the upper part of the feather has then gone ; and even if left for a few days after this has happened, the point will be found much injured, and the value considerably reduced.

It is to enable us to take the feather at its prime,

without injuring the next growth, that cutting the feathers after six months' growth has now become an universal practice as regards the quill feathers—that is, the white and long grey, or what naturalists call the primary, secondary and tertiary feathers—the stumps being left in till ripe.

As regards the blacks and tails, the practice varies considerably. The best plan is :—When the chick is seven months old, cut the quill feathers as near the wing as you can without letting the stumps bleed; pull out two rows of the brown feathers above the quill, also two rows above and below the arm of the wing, taking care not to pull so many as to leave the skin exposed, nor yet to take the floss feathers, that is, the row of light feathers next the leg, which are of little value and greatly help to keep the bird warm. Pull out the tail. Two months afterwards pull out the quill stumps. Six months after this you repeat the process, leaving the quill feather stumps in two months each time. You thus have after the first plucking a growth of eight months for the black and drab feathers, which is no injury to them, as their points are not liable to get damaged, and they protect the quill feathers for the first four months of their growth.

The tail is quite ready to pull every seven months, and this is the best thing to do; if left till the time

comes to cut the quill feathers, it is much damaged.
But if the symmetry of the bird is desired to be kept by
having all its feathers ripe at one time, then the tail
should be cut and stumps drawn, as with the quill
feathers.   But with breeding birds the stumps in the
hen's tail are apt to baulk the male in pairing.

Great care should be exercised in pulling the brown
feathers from the young birds at the first plucking, as
the skin and flesh are very tender, and the socket is apt
to pull out, when a blank will be there for ever.   To
avoid this, the flesh should be held down with the fore-
finger and thumb of the left hand.

In drawing the quills after leaving them the two
months, it will be found that they are still a little
moist and slightly bloody, but it is better not to leave
them longer, or the new feather will have begun to
grow, and sometimes will be pulled out, having adhered
to the old quill.   This I believe to be the cause of blanks
in the wing, which every Ostrich-farmer must have
experienced.   I do not speak positively as to this being
the cause, but I never remember noticing blanks when
I used to pluck every bird at six months old, and
regularly every six months afterwards.

Once in the early days I was busy plucking some
chicks six months old, when another of the first beginners of bird-farming happened to pay me a visit.   He

was dreadfully shocked at the idea of plucking a chick under a year old. Seven months afterwards I had plucked the same birds again, and sold the feathers, netting £7 10s. a bird. With this money I went up in the Karoo country to try and purchase more birds, when I came to my friend's house. We visited his young birds, rather older than mine, and found, in the place of a nice young crop of feathers, he had half blanks in nearly every bird, and the remainder twisted and bad. Of course, other causes may have had something to do with this, but as the birds were in good condition I have no doubt that the pulling out of the young feather which was adhering to the old one was the main cause.

It is quite possible that there is something to be learnt yet about taking the feathers, and that cutting the quill allows the air to penetrate down the stump and causes it to shrink, and consequently that the socket is not kept as wide to allow of the growth of the new feather as in the ordinary course of nature, when the old feather remains in perhaps for years, and is gradually pushed out by the new feather.

It is self-evident that the tame feather is not nearly so heavy or long as the wild one, but then it must be borne in mind that the Ostrich has no moulting season, it only sheds a feather now and again; consequently the whole growing strength is thrown into a very few

feathers, whilst with the tame bird it is divided amongst
the whole of the quills.

This is another reason why it is better to pull the
other wing feathers when the quills are cut; the quills
then get the whole growing power for their last two
months, when the blacks have ceased to grow.

For a large troop of birds, say 150, the best kind of
plucking-box is a kraal in a fence, made of yellow wood
planks nailed on to quartering, and this quartering
should be bolted on to sneezewood feet. The size of the
kraal should be twenty feet square and five feet high,
one foot being left open at the bottom. There should be
two plank doors on hinges opening on either side of the
fence; alongside this kraal, and communicating with it
by a sliding door should be another kraal, only ten feet
wide, with one end moveable, and made of lighter timber, say three-quarter-inch deal: this latter kraal should
also have two doors opening in different directions.

The birds having been got into the large kraal, those
that are wanted to be plucked or branded are picked out
and put into the small kraal. The moveable end of the
small kraal is brought down and the birds jammed up,
when the men can stand in amongst them and pluck
with the greatest impunity, one man standing outside
to receive the feathers. For breeding camps, a simple
kraal eight feet square, with one end moveable, is suffi-

cient. A bottom along the back of the moveable end, for a man to stand on, avoids the necessity of his going in to the birds.

The best implements for cutting the feathers are the pruning-scissors with two bends in them. For drawing the stumps little sixpenny pincers are the best.

In pulling the stumps or feathers, care should be taken to make the man stand well behind the bird, and draw them straight out.

# CHAPTER XIII.

## PREPARING THE FEATHERS FOR MARKET.

Washing the feathers has been much in vogue of late years, and although at first the producer undoubtedly got a better price by doing so, the dealers are no longer misled by the showy appearance thus given to the feathers, but buy them by their quality, giving the preference to the unwashed article. The washed feather is apt to discolour on the voyage, and the manufacturers greatly prefer doing the washing themselves. The only feathers the grower should wash are old feathers that have got soiled and would spoil the look of the others, and occasionally tails that are heavy with mud.

I shall, however, later on describe the best process for washing feathers, as the farmer should undoubtedly know how to do it, so as to prepare feathers for shows or other purposes.

We will suppose that whilst plucking, the cocks wings, the hens' wings, cocks' tails, hens' tails, blacks and drabs have been kept separate, and have been taken to a room with tables in it. The sorter will first take in

HEATHERTON FEATHER ROOM.

hand the cocks' quill feathers ; these he will—feather by feather—sort first into heaps consisting of prime whites, first whites, second whites, tipped whites, best fancy-coloured, and second fancy-coloured. He will then take each one of these heaps separately, and sort each kind into six or more lengths ; he will then proceed to tie them up in bunches according to their lengths, about twenty quills of the longest making a bunch, and rather more of the shorter ones. The second whites can all go into one bunch. The tipped whites are whites with black tips.

The hens' wings he will first sort into heaps according to their shades of colour, with a second quality heap for each shade, and then again sort each heap into lengths as with the whites. Amongst the hens' feathers he will get some white ones, but these have not the gloss of cocks' whites, and should be kept separate. The hens' wings require more judgment and care in sorting to make the best of them than any others.

The hens' tails he will sort into six heaps, as follows, and then tie up. The heaps will be :—First, whites ; second, light-coloured ; third, coloured ; fourth, dark-coloured ; fifth, short ; sixth, broken feathers. The cocks' tails into seven heaps, namely :—three lengths of whites, one of broken feathers, and three lengths of what are called mixed tails, that is, white tails with black butts.

G

The blacks and drabs should each be run into seven
different lengths, with a bunch each of broken feathers,
and one each of floss. The floss are the soft feathers
that should not be plucked, but of which there are
always some taken by accident. Care should be taken
that any old chicken feathers that may get in amongst
them are carefully removed, as these greatly spoil their
value.

The various heaps of blacks and drabs should be tied
into bunches, the size being regulated by the number
that can be conveniently held in the hand; they should
then be tied three or four together, with the exception
of the long blacks and drabs, which are better in small
bunches. It will then be found that they will nicely
divide into—First, long; second, medium; third and
fourth, two qualities of shorts; fifth, broken feathers,
and the sixth floss.

The chicken feathers will sort into five qualities :—
First, white chickens', which can include any with a
slight colour ; second, light-coloured chickens' ; third,
coloured chickens' ; fourth, chickens' tails ; fifth, dark
chickens'.

The sorter, having now got all his feathers tied up,
should proceed to arrange his lots as he intends them
to be sold. He should then frame a list, and ticket
each bunch with his name and the number of the lot

it belongs to. As a sample I give my last sale, the lot fetching £545, prices being at the time the lowest known for years.

| No. | Bunches. | Description. | lbs. | ozs. |
|---|---|---|---|---|
| 1 | 24 | Prime white | 4 | 15¾ |
| 2 | 5 | ,, ,, | 1 | 2¾ |
| 3 | 3 | ,, ,, | 0 | 12 |
| 4 | 5 | ,, ,, | 1 | 2½ |
| 5 | 4 | ,, ,, | 0 | 11¼ |
| 6 | 2 | ,, ,, | 0 | 6 |
| 7 | 4 | First ,, | 0 | 13½ |
| 8 | 1 | ,, ,, | 0 | 6¾ |
| 9 | 2 | Fringed ,, | 0 | 13 |
| 10 | 2 | ,, ,, | 0 | 7 |
| 11 | 3 | Seconds ,, | 0 | 10¼ |
| 12 | 1 | Tipped ,, | 0 | 2¾ |
| 13 | 1 | Fancy-col$^{d.}$ | 0 | 4¾ |
| 14 | 1 | ,, ,, | 0 | 8¼ |
| 15 | 1 | ,, ,, | 0 | 5½ |
| 16 | 3 | Long col$^{d.}$ light | 0 | 12¼ |
| 17 | 2 | ,, ,, ,, | 0 | 9¼ |
| 18 | 4 | ,, ,, ,, | 0 | 10¾ |
| 19 | 1 | ,, ,, ,, | 0 | 4¼ |
| 20 | 1 | Long col$^{d.}$ dark | 0 | 8½ |
| 21 | 1 | Long col$^{d.}$ seconds | 0 | 9¾ |
| 22 | 7 | White tails | 1 | 14½ |
| 23 | 1 | Damaged white tails | 0 | 2 |
| 24 | 4 | Mixed tails | 0 | 8¾ |
| 25 | 4 | Light ,, | 0 | 14½ |
| 26 | 1 | Col$^{d.}$ ,, | 0 | 4¾ |
| 27 | 4 | Long blacks | 2 | 4 |
| 28 | 15 | Medium ,, | 6 | 15½ |

| No. | Bunches. | Description. | lbs. | ozs. |
|---|---|---|---|---|
| 29 | ... 22 | Short    ,,    ...      ... | 8 | 7½ |
| 30 | ... 2 ... | Floss    ,,    ...  ...  ... | 1 | 1 |
| 31 | 1 | Long damaged blacks ... | 0 | 1¾ |
| 32 | ... 5 ... | Long drab  ...  ... | 3 | 0½ |
| 33 | ... 7 ... | Medium ,,    ...  ...  ... | 3 | 13 |
| 34 | ... 9 ... | Short    ,,    ...      ... | 3 | 7 |
| 35 | ... 1 ... | Floss    ,,    ...  ...  ... | 0 | 9 |
| 37 | ... 1 | Damaged long drab  ... | 0 | 2¾ |
| 36 | ... 8 ... | Inferior short    ,,    ... | 3 | 10 |
| 38 | ... 41 ... | White chickens'  ...  ... | 6 | 12¾ |
| 39 | 17 ... | Light colᵈ· ,,      ...  ... | 3 | 0¾ |
| 40 | ... 11 ... | Colᵈ·        ,,      ...  ... | 1 | 10½ |
| 41 | ... 3 ... | Chickens' tails  ...  ... | 1 | 14 |
| 42 | ... 18 ... | Dark chickens'    ...  ... | 7 | 14 |

The numbers are given here to show all the whites together, and then the feminas, &c.; but in sending them to market it is better to arrange the numbers so that a lot of whites are followed by a lot of feminas, then a lot of whites again, then a lot of fancy colours, then whites again, and so on right through. This assists to keep the lots from being mixed upon the sale-tables, and insures the buyers seeing clearly which lot they are bidding for.

It cannot be too strongly impressed on the sorter not to put broken or inferior feathers with the good ones; not only as it is not honest, but it defeats its own end: the buyer buys nearly as much by the feel of the feather as by the look. He takes the bunches in one hand, and presses on the top of the bunch with the other; if there is a broken feather in the bunch it is at once felt.

Every Ostrich-farmer should weigh his feathers before sending them to market. He can buy agate beam scales, including a set of weights, for £2, which a single feather will turn. The weights, however, must be assized, as there is no depending on them as sold.

The sorter should avoid making an unnecessary number of lots, as each lot has to turn the scale, causing a loss in many lots of nearly a quarter of an ounce.

### FEATHER WASHING.

This is a very simple process, and can be done by the black women, but it requires careful supervision. Have two baths, put in a little washing-soda, shred into the one about a quarter of a pound of soap, and pour boiling water upon it, stirring until it is dissolved, to make a strong lather; in the other bath put half the quantity of soap, to make a weaker lather. When the hand can be borne comfortably in the water, take a few feathers and rub them well with the hand against the side of the bath, taking care to rub towards the tip of the feather. When the dirt is pretty well out, wash them in the same way in the second bath, then plunge them into clear cold water to get all the soap out, then in blue water about the same strength as you use for clothes. Wring them out well, and finally put them through thick starch (the starch simply mixed with cold water).

The feathers must then be shaken in the hand, out of doors in the sun and wind, until perfectly dry, when they should look snow-white.

# CHAPTER XIV

We have considered in the last chapter the preparing of the feathers for the Colonial market. But the farmer who would be thoroughly successful should use every endeavour to know as much as possible of the home markets and the final retail market, where the goods pass from the shopkeeper to the wearer. Since our arrival in England we have made it our special work to acquaint ourselves with all these, by attending the public sales, and by becoming acquainted with some of the largest shopkeepers who dress and dye the feathers, and keep shops for the sale of these articles only.

As most of my Cape readers are aware, the greater part of the Cape feathers are bought up and exported by a very few men, and of these by far the largest buyers are the resident representatives of the few great English manufacturers; where the ordinary merchant has tried exporting feathers it has generally resulted in a loss. The reason has generally been considered a mystery, but there is no mystery about it. These men have enormous connections in many parts

of the world. The feathers as bought are all assorted
abroad into cases adapted for the different markets,
packed in tin-lined cases, or cases lined with prepared
paper, sewn up in canvas, and shipped to England.

The English sales are held monthly. The principal
auctioneers are Messrs. Lewis & Peat, and Hale & Son;
the feathers catalogued by them at this month's sale
consisting of 590 cases, with a net weight of 15,769 lbs.
The cases on arrival are warehoused at the warehouses
in Billiter Street, where they are opened, and the
feathers exposed on tables with wire divisions to separate each lot, one long table under the windows being
reserved for intending purchasers to examine the
feathers on. The warehouses are open for a few
days before the sale, and intending purchasers go
with their catalogues, the great dealers examine and
fix their valuations on every case, the smaller buyers
only valuing those cases that are likely to suit their
wants. On entering the warehouse the visitor is taken
in charge by one of the attendants, who remains with
him as long as he is in the building, and carries any
lots he wishes to examine from the feather tables to the
table under the windows. The sales are held at the
"Commercial Sale Rooms," Mincing Lane; but we
cannot do better than give the notice and conditions
as published on the catalogues, viz. :—

# For Public Sale,

## BY LEWIS & PEAT

### AT THE

## LONDON COMMERCIAL SALE ROOMS,

### On Wednesday, May 18th, 1881,

### AT ELEVEN O'CLOCK,

#### THE FOLLOWING GOODS, VIZ. :—

| 350 Cases 1 Parcel } | OSTRICH FEATHERS |
|---|---|

## LONDON PRODUCE BROKERS' ASSOCIATION'S PUBLIC SALE CONDITIONS.

### CONDITIONS.

1.—The highest bidder to be the purchaser; and if any dispute arise the lot shall be put up again, or settled by a show of hands, unless left to the decision of the Selling Broker.

2.—All Brokers who do not declare their Principals in writing within three days after the sale, and those who may purchase for Principals not satisfactorily known to the Selling Broker, will be held responsible as the Principals, and obliged themselves to pay for the goods so bought. The biddings of parties who have been defaulters at previous Sales will not be taken.

3.—Goods to be taken at Dock original working weights, with all faults, errors in count or description, as they now are in the Warehouses, where they will be considered at the risk of the Sellers against fire (to the amount of the Contract value only) until the prompt day, unless previously paid for.

4.—Prompt as printed. Payment on delivery of warrants or order, if required.

5.—Lot money as customary, to be paid to the Selling Broker, whether bought at or after the Sale. Buyers to pay rent from the expiration of the prompt, with re-housing or re-warehousing.

6.—In the event of the non-fulfilment of the Sale Conditions, the Goods may be re-sold immediately, either by Public Sale or Private Contract at the option of the Selling Broker, and all losses, charges, interest of money or any other damage that may arise, shall be made good by the defaulted and for which he will be liable to be sued.

Prompt Fourteen Days.    Without Discount.

The feathers are put up at per lot as catalogued, the
bidding being in advances of £2 10s. a bid on the larger
lots, and £1 a bid on the smaller cases.   The auctioneer
sits on a raised dais, with two assistants on either side,
the company being in front of them on seats rising tier
upon tier.   The chief assistant generally starts the lot at
something far below its value, as, for instance, a case
worth £250 he will start by crying out, " £150 on
my side ; " the assistant on the other side catches a
look from a buyer, and shouts, " 52 10 my side ; "
the other assistant catches a sign from a bidder—
perhaps nothing more than a sign with his penholder—
and shouts, " 55 my side ; "   and so on, till the
bidding stops, and the lot is knocked down, when the
assistant who got the last bid shouts out, " My buyer,"
or some such expression, and writes down his name in
his list.   In no case is the name of the purchaser
disclosed.   To prevent mistakes, especially where two
bidders are sitting close together, the assistant who took
the last bid gives a glance at the man he booked the lot
down to, and gets an answering glance back to make
sure he is right.   A great many lots are bought in,
and the old hands in many cases know when it is so,
and pass their remarks freely.

Judging from what I have seen, I should say very
few of our best feathers ever go on the public sales, and

that the principal reason why the ordinary Cape merchant loses by exporting feathers and selling them on
the London sales is a want of knowledge in making
up the cases to suit the retail dealer. Taking the lot
I here give out of the catalogues—

Ex " Trojan "

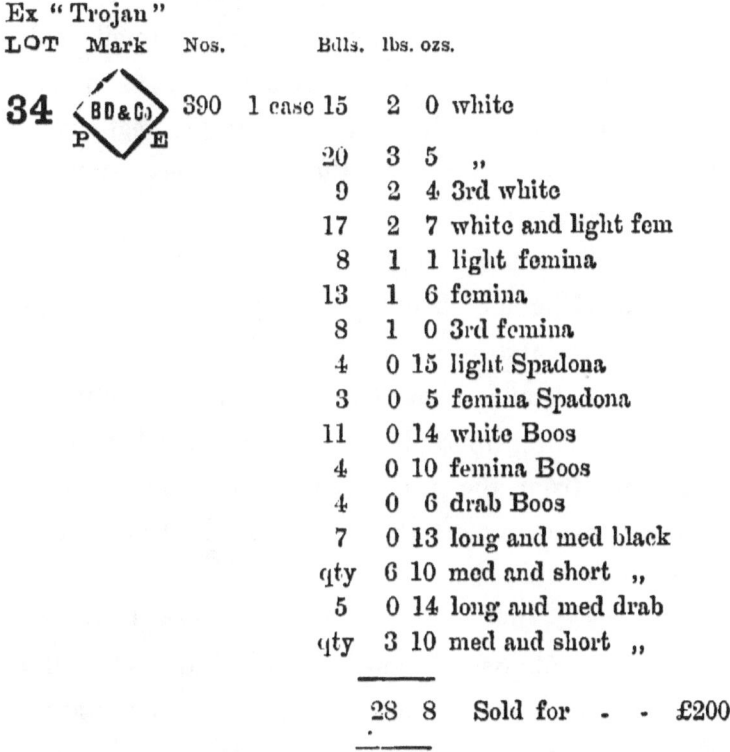

| LOT | Mark | Nos. | | Bdls. | lbs. | ozs. | |
|---|---|---|---|---|---|---|---|
| 34 | BD&Co P E | 390 | 1 case 15 | 2 | 0 | white | |
| | | | 20 | 3 | 5 | ,, | |
| | | | 9 | 2 | 4 | 3rd white | |
| | | | 17 | 2 | 7 | white and light fem | |
| | | | 8 | 1 | 1 | light femina | |
| | | | 13 | 1 | 6 | femina | |
| | | | 8 | 1 | 0 | 3rd femina | |
| | | | 4 | 0 | 15 | light Spadona | |
| | | | 3 | 0 | 5 | femina Spadona | |
| | | | 11 | 0 | 14 | white Boos | |
| | | | 4 | 0 | 10 | femina Boos | |
| | | | 4 | 0 | 6 | drab Boos | |
| | | | 7 | 0 | 13 | long and med black | |
| | | | qty | 6 | 10 | med and short ,, | |
| | | | 5 | 0 | 14 | long and med drab | |
| | | | qty | 3 | 10 | med and short ,, | |
| | | | | 28 | 8 | Sold for - - £200 | |

the first, fourth, fifth and tenth lines might suit a
west-end retailer, whilst he could do nothing with the
other lines; whilst a retailer from a manufacturing

town might do with the cheaper lines, but could do nothing with the best lines. Or in the lots made up of one kind of feather only, the quality in the same case varied so much that only in exceptional cases could the same retailer make use of all the feathers it contained.

The consequence of this is, to play directly into the hands of middlemen by keeping the retail dealer out of the public sales, and leaving it to middlemen to buy there, and, by re-sorting the feathers, to suit the retail dealer with the article his particular locality consumes.

It would be much to the advantage of the Ostrich-farmer if Cape merchants generally would study this subject more, and learn how to make up cases to suit the various retailers, so that they would acquire the habit of coming more to the London market instead of buying from the middleman, whose profits mean so much taken out of the pockets of the Cape farmer and merchant.

The great complaint against our Cape feathers is a want of fulness, closeness, and breadth of fluff of the lower part of our feathers, as well as a want of weight at the tip. But we have seen many parcels of Cape feathers that would compare favourably with the best Barbary feathers, and if this complaint against our feathers were more generally known by

## THE AUTHOR'S PRIZE FEATHERS

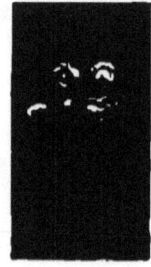 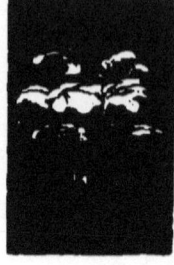  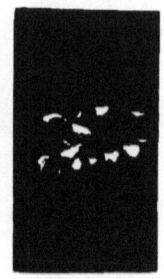

our growers, selection of the breeding birds would soon remedy it. At the present time the demand is not so much for length of feather as for this fulness of fluff; and the immense difference this makes in the value of different parcels to the retail dealer can be readily seen when we consider that with thin feathers it will take three—one on the top of the other—to make a good hat-feather, whilst with thick feathers it will only take two.

The present fashions all run on light dyed feathers, such as orange and blue, the colour being deep at the base and gradually getting lighter at the top, white feathers being scarcely worn at all. Within the last few months a process has been discovered by which the natural colouring of our femina and fancy-coloured feathers can be extracted, and there is an establishment in London where you can send feathers and have the colouring removed for £5 a pound. It is this that has caused the great drop in white feathers, whilst dark goods have kept up their price.

We personally supply several dealers in different parts of the world with feathers, either grown by ourselves or bought from other growers. Anyone interested in feathers can communicate with us.

# CHAPTER XV.

THE young beginner should avoid buying at large sales which are constantly held in the towns all over the colony. They are nearly all birds bought up cheap by speculators, owing to some fault, and the most bare-faced swindling is practised. I have heard of more than one case of men buying guaranteed breeders, where they have both turned out cocks. And where you see birds advertised as being four and five years old, they are seldom more than two-and-a-half to three-and-a-half years. Yet the prices given at these sales are generally in excess of what the beginner would give if he went to some well-known breeder, whose word he could perfectly rely on, and got a pair of good breeders that would probably have a nest within a month or two.

The men that should buy at these sales are men in large way, with great experience, but these are just the men that are the most chary. Of course, these remarks on sales do not apply to farmers' stocks being sold off, or when the birds are known. The present price of a good pair of guaranteed breeders—that is, a pair that have been breeding together—is about £200, but the beginner should get birds that have not only had one nest, but should, if possible, get birds that have bred for two or three seasons, and have had not less than three nests each season. He may not always be able to get guaranteed breeders, in which case he should buy good four-year-old birds, which he should get for £100 to £130 a pair. If they have been well nourished as young birds, and are well forward, the cock with a deep scarlet in front of his legs and round the eyes, and the back sinews of the leg pink, with generative organ thoroughly developed, and that of the hen large, soft, and sticky, he can then pretty safely rely on their breeding that season.

The term "guaranteed breeders" is so universally used now to designate birds that have had nests, that any purchaser who had bought birds sold under this designation, without any further questions being put and answered, and which he could afterwards prove had never bred, would have no difficulty in law in recovering full damages. But supposing an unscrupulous person to sell as "guaranteed breeders" two birds, both of which have bred, but not together as a pair, it might be doubtful if the purchaser could recover damages; so it is always advisable to put the following questions. On the answers given, a good idea could be formed of the value of the pair as breeders:—

1. What age are they?

2. How many years have they been breeding together?

3. How many nests have they had each year?

4. How many eggs do they average in each nest?

5. How many of these nests have they sat out?

6. What average of chicks do they bring out?

7. Are their chickens strong and healthy?

Of course many large breeders could not answer these questions categorically, but they would then give a general character of the pair, whether good, fair, or indifferent breeders.

With regard to the first two questions, our experience is that the older the better. We have birds that we know to be over sixteen years, and they breed more freely, sit more steadily, and bring out a larger percentage than any birds we have.

Three-year old birds will sometimes breed (especially the hens), but no reliance can be placed on their doing so; and if they do, I should doubt its being good either for them or their progeny.

The common difficulty of getting a young pair to breed is, the cock gets so excited and furious that the hen becomes timid and runs from him. Holding the hen's head and covering her eyes is often resorted to for the first few times, and with success. Another good plan is, to take the cock away for a short time to a strange camp. This tames him a little, and when taken back he is generally all right. But on no account ever take the hen to the cocks' camp.

In choosing the birds you will, of course, be largely influenced by the quality of the feathers. It has been the fashion to run entirely after white-feathered hens, with not half enough regard as to the quality of the feather in other respects. Dark hens' feathers of good breadth, softness, closeness and droop are worth far more than indifferent hens' feathers that are white. The dark hen will transmit her good qualities to her cock progeny, and benefit the future pluckings far more than would the whiteness of the light hen's feathers, if inferior in other respects.

The birds should also be selected for coming from a good breeding strain. They should have a well-developed, muscular frame, large feet, thick, powerful-looking legs, with great depth of girth, and a prominent, bold eye. On no account have anything to do with a herring-gutted, flyaway-looking bird.

The body feathers should be curly, rich in colour, with a shiny gloss on them; and the birds, if in good condition, should be broad across the back, with a slight

H

furrow running down the middle. The tamer and
more thoroughly domesticated they are the better, but
by tameness I do not mean that they should not be
pugnacious.

Avoid selecting brothers and sisters, especially if
from the same brood or the same season; for although
I doubt there being any proof forthcoming as yet that
any weakness in the chicks can be traced to this cause,
still it is beyond doubt that all sorts of undesirable
results have ensued from in-breeding in other animals;
and, as like begets like, if there is a tendency to weakness in any organ running in a family, every time
members of that family inter-breed, this weakness
will be more highly developed. But, above all, the
marked checks that nature puts on the Ostrich inter-
breeding in the wild state should make us careful. The
first of these checks is, the hen invariably coming into
season earlier than the cock, and the persistent efforts
she makes at this time to get away from the camp she
is in, and to wander far distances until she meets some
strange cock. The second is the timidity of the birds,
which in a wild state must cause the broods to be
constantly dispersed before they come to maturity.

The size of the camp for a pair of birds greatly
varies. The best are from twenty to forty acres each
in Karoo country, but smaller on the coast, the birds

feeding themselves entirely, except in very severe droughts, when they will get daily 1 lb. of mealies and some prickly pear leaves cut up.

In this manner they cost hardly anything to keep, they breed freely, keep healthy, sit steadily, and have nearly every egg fertile. The only objection is the amount of ground required—which is not often of much consideration in Africa—and the cost of fencing; but this is made up immeasurably by the after-saving.

Others, again, will have them in tiny camps down to forty yards square; of course, then they must be entirely artificially fed, and their breeding will not be so certain, even supposing that they remain in perfect health, which we very much doubt.

The breeding birds need not have water at all if the camps are large and the herbage at all succulent, such as the Karoo veldt. We know many breeding birds that have not had water for years, and of those that have access to water some do not avail themselves of it ; but we prefer growing birds to have free access to water.

If the camps are large, they do very well abutting on to each other, even if there is only a wire fence dividing them; as, when once the cocks get used to each other they scarcely ever bother to fight, they get to know which is master, and the conquered one keeps away

H 2

from the other's fence. But when the camps are
small, they bother up and down after each other all
day.

There should always be a supply of crushed bones
in each camp ; and on sour veldt an occasional supply
of salt is advisable.

The fact of the birds having paired is known by the
cock leaving an unmistakeable mark on the left side of
the tail. The oftener it has been done the more conspicuous becomes the mark.

Many breeders get their birds so savage that they
are hardly manageable : this is from want of care or
knowledge. If men are allowed to enter the camps
with bad bushes, and the birds get fighting with them,
or, worse still, if they go with none at all, and then
dodge about, the quietest bird will in a week or two be
made perfectly rampant. But if good bushes are taken
the bird gets to know that he can do nothing, and
seldom attempts any nonsense. If they are always
treated like this, on a pinch a man could walk through
the camp with only a walking-stick held out, and they
would not charge ; though if he had nothing in his hand
they would.

# CHAPTER XVI.

EXCEPTING a few of the very lowest forms in the animal kingdom, everything possessing animate life has come from an egg; not as we see it when laid by a bird, but as such an egg would appear if stripped of the shell, the different parchment-like coverings, and the albumen. The ovary of the bird, situated under the hump of the back-bone, consists of a cluster of yolks like a bunch of grapes, the yolks being held to the stems somewhat as an acorn is held in the cup. As puberty comes on, the yolks which have been small, but of various sizes, grow rapidly, and as they reach the full size are ready to be fertilised by the male; after which they drop off, and in passing down the ovary duct, first the albumen (the white), is added to them, then the white skins, of which there are two, then the shell, and lastly the colouring, when the egg is given forth, containing within its shell all that will constitute the future bird. The germ floats on the top of the yolk, being suspended from the two ends of the egg by two spiral cords, the mechanism of which is so beautiful that no matter how the egg is turned the germ will come to the top ; and all that is required to effect the wonderful change of this mass of liquid to the natural chick with its solid bones, muscles, flesh, and vital organs, is the application of a certain amount of heat given in a certain manner.

So much the Great Creator has permitted man to discover, but what this vital spark is He alone knows. It is generally supposed to proceed from the male only, the female simply receiving it on one of her ova, and in mammals stamping her impress upon it during the period of gestation. But this can hardly be so with aves, as with these the germ so quickly leaves the female, after which she can exercise no influence over it.

The popular delusion is that the yolk contains the materials that go to compose the chick. But this is not so. The albumen contains the whole, the yolk simply feeding the embryo and the chick for the first few days after its birth ; though we may suppose that a considerable chemical change takes place, as the yolk, which was at first yellow, becomes green by the time the chick comes forth from its shell, and the yolk-sac is taken into the abdominal cavity, which closes over it. The amount of the yolk that must be consumed prior to the chick hatching must be very small, as up to that time it has only lost about one-sixth of its weight, being about the same proportion as the total loss of weight of the egg by evaporation during the time of incubation.

The yolk-sac is connected to the chick about half-way down its small intestine, and as the action of the bowels (which is always at work in every living animal, forcing everything contained in them from the head to-wards the anus) is at work previous to the chick leaving the shell, as proved by the excrement which the chick voids before leaving it, the yolk must be digested, and nourishment drawn from it by the large intestines and the lower half of the small one; the liver, the stomach with its gastric glands, and the gizzard not coming into use until the bird swallows food through its mouth. So that the popular fallacy of the bird being born with a "yellow liver," having any connection with the yellow yolk is disproved—first by the yolk, as we have seen, not being yellow at this time, and secondly, that by no possible reasoning can the yolk be supposed to enter the liver.

A certain class of philosophers, known as evolutionists, have attempted to reduce the works of the Great Creator to the action of two laws, viz., that of the "survival of the fittest," and of "sexual selection." That these two laws are in operation neither we nor any one else who watches nature can deny, but that they

are sufficient to account for all the wonderful and
beautiful things in nature which we see around us, is to
us a monstrous idea, and can only be entertained by
those who, observing the working of these two laws,
become so wrapt in them that they lose sight of the in-
numerable other laws which Providence has placed to
keep everything in the same order in which it was
created.   These men refer all the gorgeous and wonderful colouring in the vegetable kingdom to the attraction
these form to the various insectivora to settle on them,
thus carrying the pollen to the stigma; whilst they
account for the gorgeous colouring of moths and but-
terflies, and of birds, by the greater attraction which
the more gorgeously-coloured males present to the
females than do the less-favoured ones.

By the action of these laws they attempt to prove
that all the various forms in the living world have been
developed from one, or, at the most, four or five
species.   But in all their arguments they carefully
ignore the scarcely less beautiful and varied colouring
of birds' eggs, which cannot in any way be accounted
for by either of these laws, as the law of the " survival
of the fittest " would have kept all eggs to neutral tints,
or to tints closely resembling that of the surface on
which they are laid.   That occasional cases of this may
be found, we are aware ; but for every such case dozens

may be given exactly the reverse, showing these are
mere coincidences; whilst the law of " sexual selection "
can by no stretch of imagination have the slightest influence on the future colouring of the egg, as this
colouring has no connection or resemblance to the bird's
plumage.

Neither has the food on which the parent bird exists
any connection with the colouring of the egg; if it had,
carnivorous birds would always have one colour, and
graminivorous another, but such is not the case.
In the family of which we are now treating, the
Ostrich has a white egg, the most conspicuous colour to
attract its enemies; whilst the Emu, having the same
habits and living under the same conditions, has a dark-
blue egg. The colouring of the egg appears to be one
of those inscrutable ordinances of the Creator, for which
man can give no reason, as it appears to serve no purpose but that of endangering the life of the enclosed
chick, by attracting the attacks of its enemies: which is
utterly opposed to the doctrine of evolutionists, who
hold that no variation in colouring or form can exist
unless it in some way benefits the future chances of the
possessor's survival or multiplication. This it certainly
does not do whilst the chick is in the shell; and as
at its birth it casts away the shell, the colouring can
exercise no influence on its after-life.

# CHAPTER XVII.

## NATURAL HATCHING.

SOME people are prejudiced against artificial hatching, and prefer letting the birds sit. If it is intended to take the chicks away as soon as hatched, it is then an immense waste of time and condition of the parent birds to allow them to sit; and by the incubator a much larger percentage of chicks can be obtained, of equal if not superior robustness. But with the incubator experience is required; some have not a room adapted for the machine; some cannot afford to purchase a thoroughly good machine, and unless this is done they are better without one, so that natural hatching is still largely practised, though it was fast going out of date till the yellow liver disease appeared, when some farmers were driven into letting their birds sit, so that the parent birds might rear them for the first month or so, as the only way of getting over this delicate time.

Whilst some pairs will bring out nearly every egg, nest after nest, others again never bring out more than a small percentage. This is generally caused by one of

HEN BIRD SITTING.

the parents beginning to sit before the other, when it is only the last laid eggs that are not addled. In these cases, the less the birds are visited or noticed in any way the better, as also in the frequent cases (especially with young pairs) where the cock will not sit at all; this latter is, I believe, almost invariably caused by the birds being artificially fed, and the camps being near the homestead or road, or where the cock gets teased, and consequently too excited to sit.

The other great cause of failure is the nests getting full of water in wet weather. When this happens the eggs never come out well; but this with proper care should never happen. As soon as two or three eggs are laid, a round hole, two yards wide and eighteen inches deep, should be dug close to the nest, the excavated ground being thrown up in a heap, and the hole filled in level with coarse sand or gravel. A few days afterwards the eggs should be moved on to it; then all fear of rain is over. The waiting a few days before moving the eggs is to avoid the risk of the hen taking fright. Making the hole so broad is to prevent the birds throwing up dirt amongst the sand with their bills, as they invariably will do if the sand does not extend beyond their reach as they sit.

Birds vary much in their habits in sitting; some

pairs sit so closely that the eggs are constantly hot from the first to the last day, whilst others will be constantly off for an hour or more at a time, and yet bring out nearly every egg.

Some birds get very impatient, especially if there are many days between the hatching of the first and the last chick, and are apt to leave the nest before all are hatched, but the less they are visited the less likely they are to do this. But if they do abandon the nest, and the forsaken eggs appear quite cold, do not despair, because if these are put in an incubator, or even wrapped in blankets and put in a warm place, they will most likely recover.

Some pairs will let a good many chicks die in the shell from want of assisting them, whilst a good pair will break with their breast-bone all that they evidently know by instinct are fast in the shell, repeating the operation till they liberate the chick; and sometimes they will even take the chick by the head and shake it clean out of the shell.

When it is intended to let the birds rear the chicks —and, mind, we say that unless this is intended it is a great mistake to let the birds sit at all—poison should be freely laid about for some time before the brood is expected to hatch, otherwise some will be sure to be taken by cats or jackals. And after the brood has left the nest, a boy should go about with them all day, otherwise they will get very wild; and although when taken away from the old birds this wildness may appear to leave them, it has not really done so : it will show out again as they get older.

In most broods, if examined, some will be found to have a hard lump hanging to the navel. This is part of the yolk-sac that has not been taken in when the chick hatched, or was helped out by the parent bird, and the navel has contracted and left it out. In artificial hatching we always push it in, but in nature it dries up, and the chick is deprived of so much of the yolk. It will be noticed that these chicks when left to nature do not thrive at first as well as the others.

Some farmers build little huts or weather-screens over the nests, but they do not answer well, whilst the sand nests are perfect in themselves.

Many breeders consider it detrimental to take the feathers of breeding birds. As far as their inclination for breeding goes this is quite a mistake, though the feathers may help them to cover their eggs, and they are certainly beneficial to them in rearing their young. But in artificial hatching and rearing, leaving the feathers on the birds is simply a dead loss.

Beginners want cautioning, that, no matter how tame the parent birds may be, directly they hear the chicks queak in the shell their whole nature changes, becoming intensely savage, the hen being worse than the cock; they will then charge with such force that unless a man has a thoroughly good bush he might easily be killed; but if he has a really good bush with him, after a few charges the bird finds it is mastered, and tames down.

HEATHERTON INCUBATING ROOM.

(From a Photograph.)

# CHAPTER XVIII.

## ARTIFICIAL HATCHING.

A LITTLE consideration of what was known of Artificial Hatching, previous to our applying the art to the multiplication of Ostriches, will prove, I believe, both interesting and instructive to the farmer.

In nature we have only one kind of bird that does not sit on its eggs, using instead artificial heat: this is the "Megapadius tumulus," the jungle-fowl of Australia. This bird is described as making immense heaps of vegetable matter, said in some cases to be fifteen feet in height by fifty in circumference, and to be used by several pairs of birds jointly, for several years in succession. The eggs are laid singly at a depth of several feet in the heap, and the holes filled in, the requisite heat being generated by the decay of the vegetable matter, as they are observed to be made where the foliage is thick and the rays of the sun cannot penetrate. In the back parts of Western Australia, on the sandy plains, where probably the necessary amount of vegetable matter and deep shade are hard to procure, the birds lay their eggs inside great heaps of sand exposed to the rays of the sun, a coating of vegetable matter being placed round the egg only, and this probably acts as a non-conductor to save the eggs from the excessive heat of the sand by day, whilst retaining enough at night.

The artificial hatching of fowls' eggs is supposed to have been practised in Egypt for many centuries. Most books on this country profess to give us descriptions of how it is done, though some say the art is known only to one small section of the people, and is handed down by them as a close secret; which, taken in conjunction with a letter from Colonel Gordon, the then Pacha of Soudan, asking us about two years ago for particulars of our incubator, and how to work one, as he was anxious to introduce Ostrich-farming there— eggs from the wild birds being easily procurable—makes us think all published statements about it should be taken with caution. The following is Lane's description, as given in his " Modern Egyptians ":—

"The Egyptians have long been famous for the art of hatching fowls' eggs by artificial heat. This practice, though obscurely described by ancient authors, appears to have been common in Egypt in very remote times. The building in which the process is performed is called, in Lower Egypt, 'Maamal el-firákh,' and in Upper Egypt 'Maamal el-farraag.' In the former division of the country there are more than a hundred such establishments, and in the latter more than half that number. Most of the superintendents, if not all, are Copts. The proprietors pay a tax to the Government. The maamal is constructed of burnt or sun dried bricks, and consists of two parallel rows of small ovens and cells for fire, divided by a narrow, vaulted passage; each oven being about nine or ten feet long, eight feet wide, and five or six feet high, and having above it a vaulted fire-cell of the same size or rather less in height. Each oven communicates with the passage by an aperture large enough for a man to enter, and with its fire-cell by a similar aperture. The fire-cells also, of the same row, communicate with each other, and each has an aperture in its vault (for the escape of the smoke), which is opened only occasionally. The passage, too, has several such apertures in its vaulted roof. The eggs are placed upon mats or straw, and one tier above another, usually to the number of three tiers in the ovens; and burning 'yelleh' (a fuel composed of the dung of animals, mixed with chopped straw, and made into the form of round, flat cakes) is placed upon the floors of the fire-cells above. The entrance of the maamal is well closed. Before it are two or three small chambers, for the attendant and the fuel, and the chicks when newly hatched. The operation is performed only during two or three months in the year—in the spring—earliest in the most southern parts of the country. Each maamal in general contains from twelve to twenty-four ovens, and receives about a hundred and fifty thousand eggs during the annual period of its continuing open, one-quarter or a third of which number generally fail. The peasants of the neighbourhood supply the eggs; the attendant of the maamal examines them, and afterwards usually gives one chicken for every two eggs that he has received. In general only half the number of ovens are used for the first ten days, and fires are lighted only in the fire-cells above these. On the eleventh day these fires are put out and others are lighted in the other fire-cells, and fresh eggs

I

placed in the ovens below these last. On the following day some of the eggs in the former ovens are removed and placed on the floor of the fire-cells above, where the fires have been extinguished. The general heat maintained during the process is from 100° to 103° of Fahrenheit's thermometer. The manager, having been accustomed to this art from his youth, knows from his long experience the exact temperature that is required for the success of the operation, without having any instrument, like our thermometer, to guide him. On the twentieth day some of the eggs first put in are hatched; but most on the twenty-first day—that is, after the same period as is required in the case of natural incubation. The weaker of the chickens are placed in the passage : the rest in the innermost of the interior apartments, where they remain a day or two before they are given to the persons to whom they are due. When the eggs first placed are hatched, and the second supply half hatched, the ovens in which the former were placed, and which are now vacant, receive the third supply; and in like manner, when the second supply is hatched, a fourth is introduced in their place."

The descriptions by other writers on Egypt agree in the main with this; one point in which they differ, and that one on which if Lane was correct would have puzzled us much, is where he says the eggs are placed tier upon tier to the height of three tiers; now if this was the case the lower and middle tier would have a superincumbent mass of cold matter on the top of the egg, where the vital germ is, and which our experience would tell us would be fatal. But other writers say the eggs are placed simply in the ovens on some non-conducting substance ; this is as we should have supposed, for the bottoms of the eggs are thus kept cool, whilst the heat is given from above to the top of the eggs—two things, as our experience shows us, of the very first importance. The other processes, viz., that of the heat from the slow fire for the first ten days and then the reduced heat, and then the eggs moved to the upper chambers, where the heat would be given equally all over, agree also with our experience. We believe imitations of these ovens have been tried in other countries and failed; probably from the greater variableness of the climate, which we are assured is in Egypt during the incubating season very steady, it never raining, and the days and nights being of nearly the same temperature. Whether their process is sufficiently accurate for them to succeed in hatching Ostrich eggs is very doubtful.

The Chinese are said to have hatched their ducks artificially from time immemorial. The process is very different to that of the Egyptians, and is described by the Rev. J. D. Gray, in his work on "China," as follows, though it is exceedingly doubtful if any European has had the chance of thoroughly investigating it :—

"Throughout the empire there are institutions called Pao-ap-chang, in which ducks' eggs are artificially hatched in large quantities. The process of incubation as practised in such establishments is as follows :—A large quantity of rice husks, or chaff, is placed above grates filled with hot charcoal embers When heated the chaff is placed in baskets, and the eggs are laid

I 2

in it. The baskets with their contents are then taken into a
dark room and placed on shelves of lattice-work, which are
arrayed in tiers on the walls. Underneath the lowest of these
shelves several portable earthenware grates are placed, containing hot charcoal embers. In this dark and heated chamber the
eggs are kept for a period of twenty-four hours. They are then
removed to an adjoining room, where they are deposited in rattan
baskets, which are three feet high, the sides being two inches
thick, and lined with coarse brown paper. Here they are allowed
to remain for ten days. In order that they may be equally
treated, it is usual to alter their position once during the day,
and once during the night. If the servants are careful, the eggs
which in the day are in the upper part of the basket, will be in
the lower part during the night. After fourteen days they are
removed, and arranged on long and very wide shelves. Here
they are covered up for warmth with broad sheets of thick paper,
made apparently of cotton. After they have occupied these
shelves for fourteen days, hundreds of ducks burst into life.
The principal establishments of this kind in the vicinity of
Canton are at Fa-tee and Pou-tai-Sluce."

In Europe, the first to attempt artificial hatching
was Réaumur, the inventor of the thermometer. His
first attempts were with decomposing dung, something
after the style of gardeners' forcing-frames; with this
he succeeded in hatching a few. His next attempts
were with ovens, in which he was partially successful,
and in 1749 he published a book called "Art de faire
Eclaire," but he failed to make it so sure of hatching as
to be of any value, and little more was heard of it
till 1840, when Mr. Cantilo invented the Hydro-

incubator, so called from water being the medium by which an even temperature was secured. From that time to the present various spurts have been made to make it commercially a success, but these have only partially succeeded, as in England it is used mainly for hatching the eggs of game that are disturbed in the hay-fields, and as a fancy amusement. In America great efforts have been made in the same direction, but with results similar to those in England. Mr. Halsted, who seems to be recognised as the great authority there, being the inventor of their great prize-taking machine, winds up an exhaustive paper, written in 1870, with the advice, that, owing to the difficulties and ready susceptibility of the eggs to be injured by any imperfection in the hatching, it is best to let the hens sit on them for the first three days. But this is admitting that the incubators are far from perfect, as they cannot be considered a success as long as it is necessary to do this.

It was left for Ostrich-farmers, who could easily observe the habits of the parent birds, to define the amount and kind of help that the parents give to the chick when it is unable to escape unaided from the shell, and to ourselves to discover the means of telling when that time had arrived; and the great profits, that we clearly saw would accrue from the successful hatching of Ostrich eggs, gave the necessary stimulus to bring the machines to perfection. We will now treat of the first introduction of the art into Africa.

Thirteen years ago the very name "incubator" was scarcely known at the Cape; and when I imported a machine to experiment with Ostrich eggs, those that heard of it looked upon it as a mad idea. Of course I did not succeed at first; many things had to be found out: notably, the necessity of reducing the temperature towards the end of the incubation, and how to tell when the chicks were ready to come out, so as to save those that were glued fast and could not break out; and how to manage the temperature with such large bodies, and to provide for the long period of six weeks' incubation, and other niceties, which all seem very simple now they have become generally known, but which entailed many weary days of study and watching the habits of the birds to find out.

Now, as is natural, other inventors are in the field, and many kinds of incubators are made and sold in all the large colonial towns, some good, some decidedly indifferent, but all pretty well successful if the eggs are left under the old birds for a fortnight or more, and then put in the machines. But this, of course, loses half the advantage of artificial hatching; 1st, in that it is during the first few days that the birds generally spoil their eggs, as we have shown in the last chapter; 2nd, in that the great pull of artificial hatching is in making the birds lay double or treble the number of eggs they otherwise would. Twelve to sixteen is a full laying, if the eggs are left, but if they are taken away as fast as laid, and only a couple of dummies left in the nest, they will lay thirty or more without stopping. No eggs are lost, and the birds do not go out of condition, as they do if they sit a few days. But it is in starting the eggs the first few days that many of the incubators fail, and in which my trebly patented machine is universally acknowledged to beat all competitors that have sprung up.

The great mistake which is made by most who have assayed to bring out a machine, is not recognising the first great provision of nature, that of the germ being so suspended to the two ends of the egg, that no matter how the egg is turned, the germ rises to the top. To prove this, take a number of eggs and break them over a dish, and in every case the vital spot will be observed on the top of the yolk. It is one of those wonderful provisions of nature that meet us at every turn, if we could only observe them. The object is that the vital spot should be brought into contact with the heated body of the old bird, the heat being given to this part of the egg only, the under side remaining quite cold till

a late period of the incubation, when the blood-vessels
have extended right round, and the heat is circulated.
It is thus nature provides, whilst giving the necessary
heat to the germ, to avoid almost entirely any evaporation from the egg.

Now, many machines are made regardless of this,
giving the heat all over the egg, and setting up a large
evaporation. This they attempt to remedy by giving
moisture by sprinkling the eggs, or inserting drawers of
wet earth, or moist sponges, under or amongst the eggs.
But this is contrary to nature, and causes the embryo
chick to breathe an unnatural atmosphere, to the detri-
ment of its future life.

But the best proof of the comparative perfection to
which artificial hatching has now being brought at the
Cape, is the numerous testimonials sent me, of from 80
to over 90 per cent. of hardy chicks being hatched from
large numbers of eggs, taken when fresh laid and
incubated. The incubators are so constructed that the
eggs can be put in daily as laid.

In natural hatching, the birds should be in pairs,
otherwise the hens are apt to fight over the eggs and
cause loss, but with artificial hatching two hens to a
cock are best.

As an example of what can be done by artificial
hatching : one set of three birds, a cock and two hens,

during the period from 30th June, 1872, to 30th June, 1873, laid 188 eggs, which produced 133 chicks; of these 18 died, leaving 115 young birds. Of these, 74 were sold at three months old for £16 each, and allowing the remaining 41 to be worth only £12 each, we have a return of £1,676 from one set of birds. The next year the same set laid 113 eggs, producing 77 chicks, and the first six months of the third year they laid 97 eggs, producing 81 chicks, being over 80 per cent. After this the cock was killed by a rascal for his feathers. This was before my incubators were brought to anything like their present perfection. But the same price would not be obtained for chicks now, neither in the last few years would so few of the chicks be lost in the rearing.

Even if a farmer does not intend to incubate as a regular thing, he should have a machine and know how to work it; or else the first time a bird refuses to sit, or comes to grief in the middle of it, he will lose heavily.

A notion was started some time ago, by the introducers of some machines, which worked with hot water instead of lamps, that the smell of paraffin was injurious, both to the eggs and chicks: but this is utter rubbish; if anything, the smell is good for them, acting as a disinfectant, some of the most successful men we know having two or more machines working with lamps in a tiny room.

The proportion of eggs that are not fertile is much smaller than is generally supposed; as a rule, when the birds pair and lay in a nest, they may be taken to be all fertile; but hens, especially young ones, will often lay a number of eggs about the veldt before any cock has paired them.

Even with the most perfect incubator and with every attention, occasionally a batch of eggs will come out badly, the chicks being gluey and often deformed; many people fancy that the thunder affects them, but this we do not believe—we believe that the fault is in the eggs themselves, which if left to nature would have failed to incubate at all, or have died in the early stages; but with the more perfect provision of heat in the incubator they are brought to maturity.

COOLIE FEEDING CHICKS.

# CHAPTER XIX.

For the first few years little difficulty was experienced in rearing the chicks ; the principal art consisted in giving them plenty to eat. Our instructions supplied with the incubators used to be :—

"Send them out with a boy the second day after hatching, if the weather is fine, and put them where they are sheltered from the wind and there is a good supply of gravel. The third day they will pick up gravel, and when they have filled the gizzard on the fourth day, they will eat any soft green food, with which they should be supplied as much as they will eat, lucerne cut up fine being the best. They should have water once a day, but it must not be brack. Return them to the incubator at night till a month old, or if there are too many for the machine, after a few days they can be put in boxes, lying on sacks or straw, and the boxes covered over, leaving a small air-hole. If too hot they will stand up with their mouths open and wings out. They should be freely supplied with crushed bones. The third and fourth day they will eat the dung of any

larger birds if they can get it; if this is not to be had,
fresh cow-dung will do as well. For the first four
days the chick lives on the yolk that it has taken into
the stomach. In wet weather they must be kept in a
warm, light room. When two months old they can be
put in a shed at night, provided it does not face the cold
winds, and at three months old can be left out altogether, except in very bad weather. The great secret is
keeping them supplied with as much green food as they
will eat."

Such were the instructions we always supplied, and
acting up to which we used to rear nearly all the chicks,
ten to twenty per cent. being the extent of our losses,
including accidents. But a few years ago the chicks in
the up-country districts began to die in spite of every
care, every chick on a farm being often swept off. The
first we heard of their dying was on a farm in the
Middleburg district about six years ago; we then heard
no more of it till it appeared in the Colesberg district
about two years afterwards, where it became prevalent
all over the district, the Cradock district soon following;
and last year it appeared in Albany, and as far as we
know all over the colony, here and there missing a farm
for one or two seasons, but sooner or later breaking out
everywhere.

The disease has got the name of "YELLOW LIVER,"

from the post-mortem revealing a bright yellow liver if death ensues before they are three weeks old, and of a nutmeg colour with yellow spots when older. But a more descriptive name is " fever."

The greatest mortality occurs when the chicks are about a month old, but this season we have known farms where it has been very fatal at the age of two and three months. From rumours in the last two months, we suspect the same thing is occurring in birds up to nine months old, but we have not had opportunities of holding post-mortems to decide if the cause was this or the worm " Strongylus Douglassii."

The symptoms are :—The birds are brisk and show every appearance of health, till some morning they are observed to crimp their necks, to appear languid, and to constantly make a short little plaintive grunt. The following days some are observed to drop behind, and to be rapidly losing their condition ; the belly loses its healthy greenish-yellow tint, becomes pendulant and of a deep blue colour ; a white circle is observed round the eyelids ; the legs grow a pinkish skin colour and thin ; the birds sweat underneath at night, appear to feel the slightest cold, lie down much when out of doors, and huddle in the corners when indoors ; easily fall when running about, and rise again slowly ; give forth a peculiar aromatic smell from their feathers, which have a sticky feel and a dark, dirty look; generally, but not always, intense and obstinate constipation sets in. The first signs of an outbreak are often some of the larger chicks apparently protruding the anus; this Mr. Hutchins, the Colonial Veterinary Surgeon, assured me was nothing but piles, but these were quite unknown to us till this fever made its appearance. The temperature of the chick at first is the normal temperature of the Ostrich, viz., 103° to 104° Fahrenheit, but it gradually falls, till at about 95° death ensues. These are the symptoms which will never be mistaken by a farmer who has once had a taste of this fatal fever amongst his chicks. Some birds die off sharp, especially if the weather is moist and muggy, with the wind from the southward; others linger on for a long time, and a few recover and grow out fine chicks; whilst others, although they grow up, always appear delicate.

The post-mortem appearances are the colour of the liver; or, where this is not so bad, small yellow abscesses will be found on the edges of the lobes. Not an atom of fat is to be observed in the body. Dropsy of the abdominal cavity is generally highly developed; the coats of the stomach peel off with the least touch. The entrails are flabby and watery. The folds of the maniply are swollen and the cœca distended, and in these stones will be found that have escaped from the gizzard, which in health never happens. The lungs generally, but not always, show congestion. The heart is flabby and dropsical, and small ulcers will often be found on the tongue and entrance to the throat. The outside coating to the gizzard has several inflamed spots, and inside the gizzard one or more punctured and discoloured spots will be noticed; this should be borne in mind, as it is as yet an unexplained phenomenon, and may point to parasites. Such are the post-mortem appearances, clearly proving that it is no sudden disease of any one organ, but a rapid and complete break-down of the whole system.

What is the cause?

Here we must at once state that we cannot as yet write with any certainty. At first, lots of men, whose experience, probably, did not go beyond one brood, were ready enough to repeat the old story of teaching their grandmothers to suck eggs, and with the dogmatism that is the sure sign of ignorance would tell us straight off what was the cause. Some declared the chicks were kept too warm at night; others, that they were too cold; or that they ate too much, or not enough, or, *ad infinitum* of any nonsense, all forgetting that it was not likely that those who had been successfully rearing chicks for twelve years would suddenly forget all they had learnt. Others, again, laid it straight off on the parent birds, that they were inbred; whereas, by a little trouble they could have found out that the chicks of old pairs that had always been healthy and reared without difficulty were now as hard to rear as any, and that the chicks of birds where the different sexes were from different parts of the colony were as bad as any others. Some again, laid it down as a fact that artificial hatching had been at the bottom of it; whereas they could have known that the first outbreak occurred with men who had never used an incubator, and whose original stock were wild birds. Besides, I have been assured that our inland farmers find the chicks captured in the veldt from wild birds as hard to rear as the tame ones. But this latter requires confirming before much importance can be attached to the statement; if it is true, it tells against the only theory to which I have attached much importance, namely, that the mischief has been brought about by over-feeding the parent birds, especially on grain.

It was soon discovered that the birds were mere machines in one sense—that, given unlimited food of a stimulating nature, there was hardly any limit to the number of eggs they would lay; but it has been observed by others, and our own experience somewhat confirms it, that the eggs under these circumstances are not so large. We do not believe that a few months' high feeding makes any perceptible difference to the future progeny, but we do think it highly probable that the continued high feeding has gradually affected the stamina of nearly all our domesticated Ostriches, causing the progeny to be weakly and easily affected by change of weather or other unfavourable circumstances. That it is so with other domesticated animals we know. Look what puny little pups a very fat bitch has, or how weakly is the progeny of a very fat sow, mare, or cow, especially if they get very little exercise! And even with the human race, is it not notorious that the children of the upper classes, living in the lap of luxury, feeding on highly stimulating food, and taking no exercise, are born more puny and more weakly than the children of the labourer, who get food enough but not of too stimulating a kind, and sufficient but not excessive work?

If this is so, then it is for us to be contented with fewer nests, where the birds are left to sit, letting them gradually recover their condition after the eggs are hatched, and we must not, as is now almost universally the custom, force them rapidly forward again by unlimited food. Or, far better still, incubate every egg, and never let the birds get into that exhausted condition they do after sitting out; and thus, whilst getting the advantage of a large number of eggs, the necessity for stimulating food is avoided.

J

Incubating every egg was my constant practice for many years, when I never knew what it was to have any trouble in rearing. The birds were never fed and were never allowed to sit for a day. In the extraordinary increase, particulars of which I have given in the chapter on Artificial Hatching, the birds scarcely ever saw a mealie or any sort of artificial food. They had a good camp, and fed themselves entirely.

A remarkable and apparently proved fact, and one which bears strongly in favour of this theory, is that, of the chicks that die of fever, an immense preponderance are cocks.

But what is to be done when an outbreak of fever comes? will be the question on every one's lips who has had a taste of it. First, we may state that all physicking has as yet availed nothing; it has only aggravated the disease. By changing the food, and by giving them aloe and prickly pear leaves cut up fine, onion or shallot tops, every effort should be made to keep the bowels open, whilst we should avoid lowering the system either by physicking or by giving them, as some do, Epsom salts in their water to drink. Redouble the care in not letting them get wet or cold, and keep them warm at night. Do not give them boiled wheat, wet bran, or any sort of cooked food, but give them dry wheat or Kaffir corn!! Above all, see that neither the room they sleep in, nor the one they are in on wet days, has any draught in it, and is free from damp; and, if possible, get a room with a large loft above it; the chill that strikes through a level iron roof towards day-break is very fatal to them!! See that no cold wind blows on them through the doorway of the room!! Keep them out of the hot sun!! See that their food is cut up very small, and that it is not of a young, succulent growth; if lucerne, it should be in blossom!! A change on to another farm has undoubtedly proved beneficial in some cases, whilst it has failed in others. We do not think the good is in the change of air; the benefit is, that if there is any aggravating cause, such as dampness or bad housing where they are, when changed to another farm this is avoided. It is generally supposed that the system wants supporting; and such things as giving them meat and milk, or tonics in the shape of sulphate of iron in their water, peppercorns, chilies, small doses of spirits and other things, have had their advocates, who have often been loud in their cry of having found an infallible remedy; but none of these things have stood the test of prolonged experience. As is the case when any sickness becomes prevalent, and a farmer has a lot of sick animals: he gives them something, or changes their diet, and they recover. He at once rushes to the conclusion that what he did was the

J 2

cause of their recovery, when in reality it was a change
in the weather, or the natural vitality of the animals,
that effected the cure.  The good old proverb, " One
swallow does not make a summer," should be borne in
mind by all farmers.  Whilst we would be the last to
have farmers reticent in speaking of and publishing any
cure or preventative they believe would be effective or
beneficial, they should avoid the mistake prevalent all
the world over of proclaiming as a proved fact that of
which the data they go upon is insufficient to constitute
proof.

As soon as the chicks are about two months old, put
them on a field of old lucerne, if possible, and let them
pick entirely for themselves, putting them in a shed at
night.  The sooner they are left to run day and night
the better : if kraaled they will persist in eating the dry
dung ; besides, their feathers get dirty, and they never
thrive so well as birds that are allowed to run at night.
Spec boom is an excellent thing to feed them on in
dry times.

Since fever has become so prevalent, some farmers
have taken to letting the old birds rear the chicks for
the first month or two.  By this means more are lost
by accidents, and of course a great waste of the parent
birds' time is entailed ; but as yet, in the upper districts. this has succeeded excellently, though we are

informed it has not done so in the long grass on the coast. What is the secret of the old birds' success is not very apparent, with the exception of the immense amount of exercise they give them, as they keep them on the trot from daylight till dark, and expose them to the wet dews and cold in a way that would be fatal in hand-rearing. When the chicks are a few days old, a pair of birds will brood and nurse thirty, but these should be as nearly as possible of one age. There is a little difficulty when the old birds are sent back to their camp, as the young birds fret. An excellent plan is to put any old tame, lame, or other large bird with them. They will quickly take to it in the place of the parent bird, but it will not brood them, so care must be taken to house them in bad weather, and great care is required to keep them tame.

Some people have an idea that the mischief is caused by a louse, with a blue body and red legs, which fastens itself on the body of the chick, and in its ears, and that even one or two of these are sufficient to set up blood-poisoning. Now, we know that one little red tick on a good-sized lamb can cause paralysis, and eventually death if not removed, whilst its removal will cause the lamb to recover in a few hours; so that we must not be too ready to condemn this theory, strange as it appears. It is said that this louse will always be found in buildings where poultry have been, even for years afterwards, and that it is easily carried and spread into all the buildings on a farm. This louse is exceedingly prevalent on birds that sleep in dirty ill-kept buildings. And without going further than saying that it is detrimental to the health of the chick, it should be sufficient to impress upon farmers the necessity of constantly cleansing, whitewashing and disinfecting all buildings used for chicks.

The chicks should also always have access to a good dusting-ground made of dry ashes, with a little " flowers of sulphur" mixed with it; and if the chickens are found to be lousy, some carbolic powder should be sprinkled over them.

# CHAPTER XX.

In writing of diseases in Ostriches I must not be understood to lay claim to any special knowledge of the science of medicine; but in the absence of any scientific work on the subject I feel it a duty to give the results of an experience as large as anybody's, coupled with a habit of devoting some portion of my time to study, and of making post-mortem examinations on all animals that die on my own farms or on others where I can get the chance, and to place the conclusions arrived at in plain language and in a practical manner before my readers.

Would that our legislature could become sufficiently enlightened to see that it is little use to spend money on agricultural shows, and to encourage men to spend large sums on importing thorough-bred stock, whilst diseases are left rampant in the country, some of them being peculiar to South Africa; and whilst no serious effort is made to give our farmers the invaluable benefits that would accrue from the government employing at least two veterinary surgeons under the leadership of one of the great men of the day in the profession. We have

now one man, but be his abilities ever so great, how little
can he accomplish of what is needed in a vast country
such as this. At least two are wanted, one in the east
and one in the west, to study and advise on our great
new industry of Ostrich-farming—unless we would see
what are possibly preventable diseases assume such
proportions and acquire such strength that it will be too
late for science to help us much. At least one botanist
and one chemical assayist are also urgently required, to
advise in what parts the various alkalies are deficient in
the herbage and soil, without which alkalies it is pretty
well proved the Ostrich cannot continue in health.

But above all a minister of agriculture is urgently
required, who would receive all reports from the government scientists, and from farmers who notice anything
peculiar, but who now, from want of some recognised
person with whom to communicate, never give the
public the benefit of their observations; and who would
see that all information bearing on agriculture and stock
was brought out in such a way as to reach the farmers.
It seems incredible that in a great country like this,
almost entirely dependent on farming pursuits, they
should be left almost uncared for by the government.
The time is fast passing when many of our farmers,
wrapt in the egotism and prejudice that is begotten of
ignorance, believed that scientific men could not teach

them anything about how to farm. The introduction
and rapid development of new industries, and the partial
failure of old ones, has taught them the great facts : that
a man cannot go on in the same groove as his father;
that with each successive generation we must advance
to something higher and more complex, unless we are
prepared, both as individuals and as a nation, to sink in
the great struggle of the world.

The known diseases of Ostriches can be conveniently
divided into simple and complex : the simple being
those where the cause and effect are easily perceived
and directly connected, such as the eating a poisonous
plant, or stop sickness from hard and indigestible food ;
the swallowing of some sharp implement, or abscess of
some organ, resulting from a wound ; hoven or keil-
sickness, resulting from eating a great quantity of very
young grass ; overgorging with some tempting food to
such an extent that the action of the stomach is stopped;
inflammation of the lungs from a cold ; diseases of
the eye caused by a blow, &c. The complex are
those where the cause is obscure, and where so many
of the vital organs are affected as to make it very
doubtful as to which was the original seat of the
disease—as in " yellow liver " in chicks, of which we
have already treated ; or the effects of parasites, either
external or internal, where they act, not as does the

"tape-worm," by directly consuming the bird's food and simply depriving it of nourishment, but where they act by destroying, or greatly injuring, some vital organ, and thus causing a general break-down of the system, as with the "Strongylus Douglassii;" disease of the kidneys, where the cause may be either a parasite in them, the effect of a cold, of bad food, or other causes; a disease of the lungs said to closely resemble the "lung disease" (pleuro-pneumonia), of cattle, and reported to have been prevalent in the Graaf Reinet district last year, but of which we have never seen a case.

All diseases were formerly divided into two classes : namely, those that were either infectious or contagious, and those that were neither infectious nor contagious; the infectious being those that were spread by inhaling the breath or the gases given off from the skin or stool of a diseased animal, the contagious being those that were spread by the contact of some absorbent gland, such as the tongue, lips, or generating organs with a diseased animal, or with the mucus which has come from a diseased animal ; the others being all those that were not transferable from one animal to another.  But of late years it has been noticed that these terms would not embrace all diseases, and the name "communicative" has been applied to all those which, whilst neither infectious or contagious, were capable of spreading from one animal to another. As yet no disease has been observed in the Ostrich which can be pronounced either infectious or contagious, but they are highly susceptible to those which are communicative, such as internal parasites.

The digestion of the Ostrich is proverbial : pieces of iron, or even, as we have known, a small table-knife, a gimlet, and a lot of nails and pieces of wood, are readily dissolved in the bird's stomach; and yet no animal or bird has proved itself so terribly susceptible to the attacks of internal worms, finding their habitat in the stomach and intestines, as the Ostrich. To the two principal worms to which the Ostrich is subject, namely, the "tape-worm" and "Strongylus Douglassii," we have devoted separate chapters. A short time ago we were asked to go to two adjoining farms, in the grass veldt, and see two troops of birds, about a year old, that had another new worm. The birds were in good condition, and none had died, so that the nature of the worm could not be told, but hundreds of what appeared to be ova of a new tape-worm were passing out in the stools. These were full of life, and moved like caterpillars. After a few hours they turned red. The disease has only just made its appearance, so that whether it would prove very serious or not remains to be seen. Anyhow, if any one observes it, he should take it in hand with vermifuges at once, and by isolating the birds from his others, whilst feeding them up well, try and stop its spreading. With these things a stitch in time is worth doubly nine.

The other principal worm inhabiting the Ostrich is a white one, from one to two inches long, located in the cœca, and found, we believe, in nearly every Ostrich. As science has yet to decide what part the cœca play in the economy of animal nature, it is impossible to say to what extent they exercise an injurious effect on the bird. It apparently belongs to the tribe "Lumbri-coides," and is found swimming about in the liquid contained in that part. When the bird is in a low condition they become very numerous. We have known large and repeated doses of santonine given daily for a week, and the birds have improved; but how far this was due to the birds being kept up at the homestead, and consequently better fed, we cannot say.

In one instance we found two very long worms threaded under the outside skin of the gizzard, apparently "guinea" worms; but as this was some years ago, and we have not since come upon it, it does not appear that it spreads.

Birds are subject to lice in their feathers, especially when in low condition or out of health; no doubt dressings of flowers of sulphur or carbolic powder would be effective, but we have not had occasion as yet to trouble about it.

Stop sickness or constipation may be either a secondary effect of worms, or a direct effect of hard, indigestible food, fever, or deranged liver. In the former case the treatment must be aimed at the worms, in the latter there is nothing as an aperient to beat one pound of Epsom salts, with one-and-a-half ounces of turpentine, mixed with hot water and given warm to a full-grown bird, the dose being correspondingly reduced for younger ones. At the same time, in a full-grown bird, the hand may be inserted up the rectum, and the hard lump of excrement —that can often be felt—removed; whilst at the same time, and in cases where this cannot be done, an injection of some gallons of warm water and soap can be given. A simple and effective enema, consisting of a large syringe, can be bought at the chemists' in Port Elizabeth or Cape Town. There is a little difficulty in inserting it, owing to the situation of the bladder, and as long as no force is used, and the point of the syringe is kept pointing in an upward direction, no harm will be done. Croton oil, up to 30 drops for a full-grown bird, is often given, but the effect is generally uncertain, and when it acts it does so too violently. In all cases the medicine should be followed by a feed of aloe or prickly pear leaves, and the bird for some time after fed on soft green food.

Sometimes a whole lot of birds when herded will be taken violently ill from eating some poisonous plant. They will be observed stretching their necks, falling about, lying down and getting up again. Heavy losses have occurred through this, principally with middling-sized chicks. They should at once have a dose of some ounces of Epsom salts, according to their size. The Dutch are great believers in a very strong decoction of coffee and chicory, and, I have heard, with very beneficial effect.

Of diseases of the kidneys little is known. That they are subject to being affected is evident, from the bird's urine when it is out of sorts becoming small in quantity and very thick, as though lime had been mixed with it. A dose of an ounce of turpentine will generally put it to rights. A remarkable feature about the urine of ostriches is, that at times, generally in the spring, it becomes quite red. I have never heard any explanation of this, and from it occurring in birds to all appearance in good health, it need not alarm the young farmer, as it probably would do if he was to observe it in his birds without having previously heard of it.

Young birds often get a disease in the muscles of the legs, ascribed by some to rheumatism, but, I believe, it should be ascribed to the after-effects of eating some poisonous herb. The bird knocks its legs together in walking; and as it grows, and its body gets heavier, the disease gets worse, and the bird eventually loses the power of walking, and dies.

A bird will often be found to be wasting away, to have little appetite, and, if neglected, it will die. A dose of three drachms of sulphate of iron daily, with as much food as the bird can be tempted to eat, will generally work a cure; but the best thing of all we have found are the Ostrich Condition Powders sold by Mr. Wells, chemist, Grahamstown. The Horse Condition Powders prepared by Messrs. Lennon and Co., Port Elizabeth, are also very good: one to be given daily for two or three weeks.

Dropsy of the "abdominal cavity" (the belly), and of the "pericardium" (the sac in which the heart hangs), is common in the Ostrich, but in every case we have examined we have found it to be a secondary symptom, resulting either from worms, constipation, or fever, &c.; and the treatment must be aimed at removing the cause, at the same time stimulating the kidneys.

Above all, the farmer should bear in mind that "Prevention is better than cure;" that the administering of medicine to animals is always more or less unsatisfactory; that the true road to success is in studying the habits and requirements of his birds, and endeavouring to the utmost of the means he has to supply their every want; and, when he sees them falling off in condition and spirits, to change their pasture or their food.

Many doctors and scientific men do not attach very great importance to the presence of parasites in mammals, but all admit that aves are subject to sweeping epizoötic diseases directly caused by entozoa, and that their presence does not necessarily prove that the bird was previously diseased; and that, contrary to what would have been expected, the herbivorous and graminivorous birds are more subject to outbreaks than the insectivorous or carnivorous birds.

# CHAPTER XXI.

## TAPE-WORMS.

TAPE-WORMS are now nearly universal in the domesti-cated Ostrich till it attains its adult age; when, unless under exceptionally unfavourable circumstances, the bird throws off the worm by its own unaided powers.

For some years after their first domestication this was an unknown disease. It seems first to have made its appearance in the extreme northern districts, and the manner in which diseases are so rapidly spread when of a communicative nature was very clearly demonstrated in the way in which this was brought into Albany. On a neighbouring farm to my own, a specu-lator left some affected birds to rest whilst he went to seek a market for them. The owner of the farm, having never seen the disease, did not notice it till I pointed out to him the joints of the worm that were deposited on the bird's excrement, and which are now so well known to every colonist; but when I urged him to hurry the birds on elsewhere, he thought I was unduly alarmed. However, the birds in a few days were sold and moved on into the Uitenhague district; but a

K

month or two afterwards the worms appeared in my friend's birds, and from them it rapidly spread to other farms, and became general in the district.

The first outbreak of this disease in each new neighbourhood was attended with very fatal results, carrying off large numbers of birds; but now its virulence has much abated, and, with our acquired knowledge of what are the best vermifuges for this particular tape-worm, the disease is no longer much dreaded. On its first outbreak we knew a man who made a determined attempt to try and stamp it out by every month dosing the whole of his birds: his idea being that if no germs were deposited on the veldt for some considerable time, and with his farms fenced in to prevent a renewal by a fresh communication, he would be rid of it; but after some time it was discovered that the guinea-fowls, pows, corhans, fowls, and many of the small birds throughout the country had contracted the disease, and were spreading it in all directions, which of course made it impossible to stamp it out. It proved very fatal to the guinea-fowl; where there were large flocks of perhaps a hundred strong, they are now reduced to a few only.

The disease generally makes its appearance in chicks about four months old, and continues in them, more or less, till about two years old, when the birds throw it off as long as the veldt is green and food abundant. Although the worms may be in great numbers in the birds, they suffer little inconvenience from them, but when the veldt gets dry and food scarce, the bird does not get sufficient sustenance to maintain itself in health and feed the worms at the same time. The worms are located in the small intestine, where they get the advantage of consuming all the best of the food as it leaves the gizzard; so that unless there is enough to satisfy the worms and also to satisfy the bird, it at once falls off in condition, and loses that most noticeable greenish-yellow tint of the skin that is so indicative of a bird in flourishing condition. This tint of the skin is caused by a thick layer of fat underlying it. The feathers, too, cease to lie level on the bird, lose their fluffiness, and the skin shrinks; and the time has arrived when the farmer, if he would save himself from loss, must dose his birds.

The family of tape-worms is represented by many species, and of the best-known vermifuges some are better adapted to one kind than another, whilst some kinds can only be effectually dealt with by a combination of two or more. The best-known tape-worm medicines are extract of male fern, turpentine, decoctions of pomegranate-root bark, kausau, pumpkin seeds, areca nut. Formerly steel or tin filings were used;

K 2

they acted by piercing the worm, but this mode of treatment is now out of date.

It should be borne in mind that the tape-worm not
only feeds itself through its mouth, but that the whole
of its body is provided with absorbent glands that suck
in food; consequently, the longer the worm the greater
amount of nourishment its host is deprived of. This
is very important to the Ostrich-farmer; as, although
it may be doubtful whether with the vermifuges at
present known, and their necessarily more or less im-
perfect administration by the farmer, he ever succeeds in
ridding the birds of the heads of the worms, still if he
only rids them of the worms' bodies, leaving the heads
fastened on to the mucous lining of the intestines by the
two little hooklets with which they are provided, he has
done a great deal. These heads will in twenty-seven
days again have grown a body of several feet in length,
from which the joints will begin to detach themselves
and to be voided out in the stools to run their separate
course in life. Even if this is all that is accomplished,
it is much : it gives the bird a sudden start in vigour—
very observable forty-eight hours afterwards—and en·
ables it to shake off the dropsical tendencies that were
setting in, and to rapidly lay on condition. From the
inveterate tendency the disease has of showing itself
again after a month or two, we cannot believe the germs

would be again taken in so quickly in such quantities, especially where the grazing-ground of the birds is changed.

A little insight into how man contracts this disease, and how it is treated in human practice, will help the farmer to an intelligent treatment of his birds. The two common kinds found in man are the "Tœnia Solium," so called from its being found singly in its host, and the "Tœnia Mediacanelleta." The former is contracted from eating diseased pork, commonly called "measly pork;" the latter from diseased beef, or—very rarely—mutton. The pig contracts the disease by swallowing a tape-worm when scavenging, or when fed on offal; the ox, either when grazing or drinking. The worm having thus got into the entrails of its host, burrows out and into the flesh, where it takes an hydatid form and lays its eggs, which are carried by circulation all over the body, remaining the thickest under the shoulder-blade, in the lower jaw, and under the root of the tongue, and forming the familiar appearance known as measly. This flesh is then eaten, some parts of it not having been sufficiently cooked through to destroy the vitality of the eggs; and if swallowed by one whose digestive powers are favourable, the egg hatches, and the worm is developed, some persons being more susceptible to the disease than others.

In treatment, the physician, whilst determining from the joints voided in the stools which kind of worm his patient is suffering from, keeps him on a reduced diet of clear soups and slops for some days, to get the stomach and entrails completely empty, when he gives a vermifuge best adapted to the kind of worm, and follows it with a strong purgative. He then, under a magnifying-glass, examines every atom of the stools, to see if the head of the worm or worms has been passed. If so, the cure is complete; if not, and only several yards of the body of the worm has come away, leaving the head, he sets to work to build up his patient's strength again for another attempt. We have a friend whom the most learned London physicians, after several attempts, gave up as incurable, and who carries his worm to the present day, and will do so till it dies of old age—the supposed length of life of this parasite is fifteen years.

The Tœnia found usually in the Ostrich is known as the broad tape-worm, or Bothriocephalus. Dr. Becker, of Grahamstown, reports discovering in one case a Tœnia Serrata, the small tape-worm common to the dog, but this is the only case in which we have heard of it. We shall, therefore, confine our remarks to the common one. This is found in great numbers in the same host; probably fifty or more could be counted. It is either swallowed in the water, or, as we believe, with the herbage. The white spots voided with the dung are each one a perfect worm, and they may be observed on a fresh stool stretching out their heads and putting out their feelers to grasp the intestine should they have the good fortune to be swallowed by a bird; but we expect, as a rule, it is only those that get washed off the dung, and are voided in the urine, and thereby get a chance to hang on to the grass, that get swallowed.

We have tried all the vermifuges mentioned in our list, with the exception of kausau, but have found none satisfactory except turpentine and male fern.

We infinitely prefer the former: it is more certain in its action, acts at the same time on the kidneys, and is cheaper. But with them both, the line between a sufficiently large dose to be effective, and that which will cause the bird to be seriously affected, even if it is not fatal, is small; and, worse still, this line does not always seem to be the same for different lots of birds of the same age; so that it is always advisable with young chicks to try two or three, with the sized dose it is intended to give, a couple of days before physicking the lot, and observing the effect. If the dose is too large it will make them drunk, stagger in their gait, and fall about; if not fatal at the time it does not appear to do them any permanent harm. If the dose is not strong enough the joints will continue to be voided, but, of course, in any case this will continue till the dung that was in the intestines previous to the exhibition of the medicine has all been voided. The worms will not always come away; in many cases they appear to be killed and become digested with the other food, but if, after three days, the joints cease to be voided, the desired end has been obtained.

The doses we recommend are :—

### TURPENTINE.

| | | | | | | |
|---|---|---|---|---|---|---|
| 4 months' chick | ... | ... | | ½ fluid ounce. | | |
| 6 ,, ,, | | ... | | ¾ ,, ounce. | | |
| 9 ,, ,, | ... | ... | | 1 ,, ounce, F ℥. | | |
| 12 ,, ,, | ... | ... | ... | 1¼ ,, ounces. | | |
| 18 ,, bird | ... | ... | ... | 1½ ,, ounces. | | |
| 2 years and upwards | | | | 2 ,, ounces. | | |

### MALE FERN.

| | | | | | | |
|---|---|---|---|---|---|---|
| 4 months' chick | ... | ... | ... | 1½ fluid drachms. | | |
| 6 ,, ,, | ... | | ... | 2 ,, ,, F ℥. | | |
| 9 ,, ,, | ... | ... | ... | 2½ ,, ,, | | |
| 12 ,, ,, | ... | ... | ... | 3½ ,, ,, | | |
| 18 ,, bird | ... | | ... | 4 ,, ,, | | |
| 2 years and upwards | | ... | ... | 6 ,, ,, | | |

In every case the dose should be most carefully measured, for which purpose the following table will be found handy :—

1 tea-spoon = 1 fluid drachm.
2 tea-spoons = 1 dessert-spoon = 2 fluid drachms.

2 dessert-spoons = 1 table-spoon = 4 fluid drachms.
2 table-spoons = 1 fluid ounce = 8 fluid drachms.
2 fluid ounces = 1 small wine-glass.
26 ,, ,, = 1 quart bottle.
40 ,, ,, = 1 imperial quart.

The ingredients to be mixed with flour into a good adhesive consistency, and then divided into two pills. A convenient way of doing this, is to multiply the number of birds to be dosed by the quantity to be given each bird, then weigh a bath or dish, and put the quantity of ingredient required into it, adding flour till the desired consistency is obtained; then weighing the bath and all, and deducting the weight of the bath previously ascertained, we have the net weight to be divided by twice the number of birds to be physicked as the weight for each pill. Turpentine, it should be borne in mind, soon evaporates. The birds having been shut up from early the previous evening, and fasted till about eight in the morning, the first pill should be given, and three hours afterwards the second; then fast them two hours more, when they can be turned out to graze, but they should be kept away from water. We do not advise following the dose with a purgative, as is often done.

The post-mortem appearances of a bird dying of tape-worm are, with the exception that the stomach is perfectly sound, in every way the same as in the case of the Strongylus Douglassii, which will be described in the next chapter.

Although our experiments with areca nut have not been satisfactory, we should like to see it further tested in conjunction with other vermifuges, because it acts as a strong purgative, and in the short time of two hours after being given. Although quarter-ounce doses given to some four months' old chicks made them drunk, and purged them, it was quickly over without any permanent ill effects; and as an experiment we gave half-ounce doses to two five months' chicks with the same results. Now, had the same amount of drunkenness been set up with male fern, a large number of the birds would have been killed, and the others seriously weakened; whilst with the nut, about three hours saw the effect worked off, and the birds were far brisker than before the dosing. This makes us think it may yet prove a valuable vermifuge for Ostriches, but it must be given in conjunction with something else; as, in the cases here quoted, and where it would appear as much as was safe was given, all the birds were not cured.

# CHAPTER XXII.

THIS is the name that Dr. Spencer Cobbold, our greatest living authority on "Entozoa" (Internal Parasites) has given to the small worm which I discovered two years ago, inhabiting in countless numbers the stomach of the Ostrich, and which is a totally new worm to science.

Two years ago I was struck with the similarity of the symptoms described in the birds that had been dying so much in the western province, in the midland districts, and a few that had commenced to die in the eastern districts, and I seized the first opportunity that offered of making a post-mortem examination of some birds that were supposed to be dying of stop-sickness, when the cause was soon discovered to be these worms being in swarms in the inner folds of the stomach, and especially on that part which contains the gastric glands; so that the whole of the gastric juices, without which no digestion can go on, were being consumed by them, and the glands themselves seriously injured.

The worm is about a quarter of an inch long, it buries

its head in the mucous membrane, which becomes greatly
swollen, and, when the birds have got the disease badly,
the inside of the stomach assumes a rotten appearance :
the worms are quite white, but appear red from the inflamed state of the stomach.

Whence has come this scourge ?  Is it quite new to
the Ostrich, or has it hitherto existed in such small
numbers as not to have injuriously affected the bird?
We think it must be a new disease, or else it
would certainly have been noticed.   When the Cattle
Diseases Commission, of which I was a member, sat in
1876, I wrote the following lines that will be found in
the report.   How quickly the prophecy has come true :—
" The Commissioners cannot condemn too strongly the
overcrowding of birds in too small enclosures and about
the homestead, the ground becoming thereby tainted ;
and although for a few years the evil effects may not be
severely felt, the result must inevitably be the breaking-
out of diseases of an unforeseen character."   The reader
must dismiss any ideas he has about worms being
generated by the bird eating indigestible food, or any
other ideas he has that would entail the idea of spon-
taneous generation.   This worm, even as any other worm
or thing possessing animated life, was begotten by the
union of the two sexes, and was born into the world.
The two sexes may have been contained in the one

being, as is often the case with Entozoa; the progeny
may have been to all appearances a different animal,
finding its habitat in a totally different host, and only
returning to its original appearance after two or more
generations. But all this does not affect the great
fact, that every living thing has had progenitors or a
progenitor, and that every Ostrich affected by this or
any other worm, must have swallowed one or more
worms, or their larvæ, before it became so affected.
Hence we see how highly communicative all parasiti-
cal diseases are.

I should explain, for the benefit of those who do not
know anything of the natural history of Entozoa, that
the term "host" is always applied to designate the
animal or insect within which the Entozoon is living.

But it must not be supposed that the picking-up of
one or more worms would necessarily give the disease;
a bird in robust health, with its powers of digestion un-
injured, may be able to resist a considerable number
of attacks, or may be feeding on such food as will
prevent the worm getting a footing, or, if it succeeds
in this, prevent it increasing to such an extent as to injuriously affect the bird. Or it may be—and this is the
important point to which we have been bringing the
reader—that the bird is, say twenty-nine days out of
thirty, able to swallow a worm or its ova without

being contaminated ; but on the thirtieth, from some
cause or other, its digestive powers were in a fit state
for the worms to get a footing, and if some were
swallowed by the bird on that day the disease would
be contracted.

Hence, in a state of nature, although the germs of
this worm, or for the matter of that scores of others, are
in small numbers on the face of the earth, the chances
of a bird picking up a worm or its eggs at a time when
these would be able to obtain a footing, is not great.
But should it do so, the wonderful instincts with which
nature has endowed all living creatures would teach it
to seek the herbs that would assist it to battle with its
enemy ; or, should it become seriously affected, and the
eggs of the worms begin to pass in considerable
numbers on to the veldt in the diseased bird's dung and
urine, the habits of the birds in wandering over large
areas, feeding here to-day and miles away to-morrow,
greatly reduce the chance of others picking up the
eggs whilst there is vitality in them, long as is the time
that most of the kind can retain it. But should the
bird become so badly affected that its health is impaired,
the instinct of self-preservation that seems implanted
in every animal, and which causes them to attack
and drive away any of the flock that are sick, puts
a further great check on its spreading. Further, it

would, whenever suffering in general health, soon fall
a prey to the several carnivora that nature has placed
ever ready to devour the Ostrich; as it is by its speed
and general alertness that the Ostrich saves itself from
them, and in both these qualities it would be deficient
whenever it was out of health. But this is the time
when it is also most susceptible to the attack of
Entozoa, and when it is for the good of its species
that it should fall a victim to the carnivora.

But when we domesticate the bird, we deprive it
of all these safeguards which nature gave it; and
unless we substitute in their place others, gained from
a general knowledge of its habits and requirements,
and backed by the discoveries of medicines and general
science, the most dire consequences must be expected.

Now, this outbreak of worms in the Ostrich I
believe has been brought about, in the first instance,
by birds being kept on veldt where the necessary
alkalies and other constituents of the herbage absolutely
essential to them are wanting. The birds then become
a prey to these worms; they commence to die,
and are moved to another farm, where they are
mixed with others possibly in good health : but
the diseased birds begin depositing the eggs in such
quantities that the others are taking them in all day,
and the first day the hitherto healthy ones are a little out

of sorts they contract the disease; and so it has gone on spreading, the germs being scattered in such quantities that even birds under the most favourable circumstances cannot escape, as the natural herbs that would have proved a sufficient antidote for ordinary attacks are not strong enough to resist them when multiplied a hundredfold.

This worm can be found in the chicks, even at six weeks old, and has proved very fatal to them at four months, and from that on to three years. Whenever a scarcity of food prevails, or the veldt gets dried up, and they are not supplied with green food, the worm seems to multiply rapidly, and if the birds are neglected fatal results will ensue.

I believe cases have been known of birds over three years old being affected; but our observations go to show that where the birds are well cared for, and are on suitable soil, they throw off these worms as they do the tape-worm when they approach the adult age. Where the contrary is the case, we suspect the soil or the conditions of life are unfavourable.

The symptoms of the birds being affected are: a falling-off in condition, drowsiness, ruffled feathers, &c., the same as described with tape-worm; but a marked feature that generally distinguishes between the two is, that in this case the bird rushes greedily at its mealies, eats a few mouthfuls, and then turns away, evidently in pain as the food enters the stomach; repeating the operation again and again till he finally leaves the mealies; but this symptom will only be seen when the bird has been suffering for some time, and to a considerable extent, when it will also often retch from the pain and throw the grain up again. If the dung be examined, it will be noticed that much of the food has passed through undigested.

In the "post-mortem" appearances: the body will be found fearfully emaciated; dropsy of the abdominal cavity will be found highly developed, as also of the pericardium, and the heart will be flabby; the small intestine and the cœca will be found full of water. In the latter will generally be found a quantity of the stones that should be in the gizzard, and ought never to leave it as long as the bird is in health. This, no doubt, is caused by the muscles of the whole body becoming relaxed, and the rings of muscles that surround the outlet of the gizzard into the small intestine being no longer able to prevent (as in health they would) the passage of anything but the finest-ground food. We have already remarked upon the appearance of the stomach.

*Treatment.*—Give the birds an extended scope of grazing-ground, and change it frequently, if possible.

L

Feed highly, using wheat, Kaffir corn, or barley, in preference to mealies; or if mealies must be used, crush them first. If the rains are plentiful, and the veldt keeps in good order and is adapted to the birds, there is no need to employ medicines, except for any birds that are very bad. For these "flowers of sulphur" has been used, with every appearance of much advantage, in doses of a table-spoonful daily for a week, and then every other day for a time; santonine in considerable doses daily is also reported to have been used to advantage, as also Wells and Lennon's Powders mentioned in a former chapter. But if the veldt is dry, besides a liberal supply of grain—say, two pounds a day per bird—they should have an unlimited supply of lucerne or cabbage, as well as prickly pear or aloe leaves cut up. We have heard on the best authority of birds, that were so far gone that they would not eat, having the above green foods forced down their throats two or three times a day and Lennon's Powders given to them, recovering and growing into fine birds. We have known turpentine and male fern to be used and beneficial effects to follow; but we think it highly probable that this was more attributable to ridding them of tape-worms than to the effect it was supposed to have had on the Strongylus. We have also heard of spirits of æther being given in ounce doses, on the theory that it

would dry up the worms, but with what results is
doubtful.   But until the discovery of some drug that
is really deadly to this worm, and at the same time
innocuous to the bird, the farmer must place his chief
reliance in keeping up the stamina of his birds, so
as best to assist nature to throw it off, and as the best
preventive to their contracting the disease.

# CHAPTER XXIII.

BEFORE considering the practicability or otherwise of emasculating the males, we should first clearly understand what objects are sought to be obtained.

Every farmer is aware of the great fact that like begets like, and consequently if an inferior-shaped, or organically faulty, or inferior-feathered bird is allowed to breed, its progeny will partake, in a greater or less degree, of the faults of the parent. Now, in a state of nature, the male Ostrich that is faulty in any of these points can get very little chance of breeding. If muscularly weak, he will be driven away by the stronger birds; if weaker than his compeers in any vital organ, he will probably ere he arrives at the age of puberty have fallen a victim to the carnivora; whilst if inferior in plumage, his chance, as compared with better-favoured birds, of attracting the hens to mate with him will be lessened. That this latter statement is true, and that it has considerable bearing on maintaining the quality of the plumage, few farmers can doubt who have watched the male bird disporting himself with every feather fully displayed to the gaze of the hen, as well as the marked preference which a hen usually exhibits for one male more than others.

But with the domesticated bird we have deprived it of the operation of this law; and it therefore becomes highly essential, if the health and beauty of the bird are to be maintained, that we should deprive the inferior birds of the power of reproducing.

This could, of course, be done by keeping all the inferior males in one enclosure, and the inferior females in another; and if no other advantages could be expected from depriving them of their breeding organs, this would be the best plan. But if we take, as an analogy, what happens with poultry when so deprived, viz., that they become much tamer, more thoroughly domesticated, grow larger, keep fat on less food, do not fight amongst themselves, are less subject to disease, and live to a greater age, we see that the subject of caponising the Ostrich becomes one of importance.

The turning of cockerels and poulets into capons and poulards is comparatively a simple matter, and is largely practised in France. The operation is performed when the bird is about six weeks old. It is first fasted for a considerable period to reduce the size of the entrails; the bird is then laid on its right side, the legs drawn back, the outer skin drawn forward, and an incision made alongside the last rib; the finger is then inserted, and the testicles or the ovary extracted, the incision then being sewn up in the usual manner.

Some years ago, in conjunction with the late Colonial Veterinary Surgeon, we made several attempts upon male Ostriches; and although we succeeded in extracting the testicles, the birds all died: the failure being caused apparently by the testicles being closely connected with the two large blood-veins that extend down the back-bone, which became ruptured in the tearing away of the testicles, which is apparently not liable to happen in poultry, the testicles being much more freely suspended.

Another obstacle to the successful operation in the Ostrich is the much smaller size of the testicles in comparison to poultry: being only about the same size in an Ostrich of two years old as in a cockerel of six weeks.

Should any of my readers feel inclined to make experiments in this line, they must bear in mind the difference of the internal construction of poultry from that of the Ostrich, which reverses the side the incision should be made upon, which in the Ostrich must be on the right side to have any chance of success. But it would be as well to draw the reader's attention to a few of these marked differences.

In the fowl, in the place of the Ostrich's stomach

we have the crop, situated under the root of the neck, the gastric glands being contained in the lower œsophagus or large pipe connecting the crop to the gizzard, which latter lies far down in the abdominal cavity; whilst the liver, which in poultry is furnished with a gall-bladder, lies on the tail side of the diagonal diaphragm, instead of on the head side, as in the Ostrich. In poultry the total length of the intestines is comparatively much shorter than in the Ostrich; what we have called the maniply in the Ostrich, and is immediately after the cœca, being altogether wanting in the fowl, the whole length of the fowl's large intestine being only a few inches.

It is quite possible that emasculation could be accomplished in both sexes by severing the oviduct, but this would require a scientific anatomist and skilful operator to perform.

Of course, as long as there is such a ready sale for all sorts of Ostriches with very little attention being paid to their quality, the subject of caponisation will not attract much attention. But the day will certainly come when none but the best birds will be allowed to breed.

# CHAPTER XXIV.

## WOUNDS.

THE Ostrich is exceedingly liable to injuries, owing to its timid nature. No matter what precautions are taken, they will occasionally injure themselves by running against fences, stumps, or into holes; whilst the habit of fighting amongst themselves causes them to give each other serious wounds. But as a set-off against this, the farmer has the consolation that their flesh heals more readily than that of any other animal we know, and is far less liable to the usual difficulty of getting wounds to heal in animals—that of being fly-blown.

Some farmers make a habit of bathing a wound either with hot or cold water directly it occurs. This is a great mistake, as nature immediately sets to work to try and repair the injury by throwing out the ingredients that go to make new flesh, which the bathing washes away. What is required is to exclude the air, at the same time uniting the parts together. Bathing should only be resorted to where dirt has got in the wound, or when the wound has not been observed for a day or so, in which case the skin will have shrunk, and the exposed flesh become hard and clotted. In this case it should be bathed for an hour or two with warm water, to soften the parts, and to allow of the shrunken skin being again loosened, so that it can be stretched over and united together in its place.

The first thing to be done is to remove any feathers that would interfere with the sewing-up, or would be likely to stick to the wound, then bring the parts of the skin together in their natural position, and stitch them up. Every farmer should have a few surgical needles, which any chemist can obtain for him at a cost of about sixpence each. If he has not these, a good-sized common needle can be used, with either common thread or waxed thread used double, or common twine used singly. The stitching is done by passing the needle through both edges of the skin, and then tying it with a double knot, cutting off the ends and repeating the operation, each stitch being separate and distinct from the other. Sufficient stitches must be used to bring the two edges of the skin completely together, which, with the pus given forth by nature from the wound, excludes the air, and this with the Ostrich in a few days effects a cure. If handy, a little carbolic oil, made of one part carbolic acid to twenty parts olive oil, rubbed over the part, keeps the flies away.

One of the worst and most awkward wounds the Ostrich-farmer has to deal with, while at the same time one of the commonest, is that to the lower part of the leg, caused by the bird getting fast in a wire or bush fence, when with its violent struggling it will often tear the flesh away, leaving the bone exposed on both sides. The skin in this part is of such a nature that it can seldom be got to unite. and the principal reliance must be placed on binding up the leg in rags dipped in carbolic oil, and keeping it so bound up for a long time until new flesh forms. But very often some of the principal muscles are severed, or so severely injured that they rot in two, and the bird loses control of its toes and eventually dies.

We have known a bird that broke its leg low down to have had a wooden leg fitted on, and to live for years ; also a very young chick that broke its leg, to have had it set with splints, and to be reared. But these are such rare exceptions, that, coupled with the immense time that must have been spent over them, they are of no practical value. In all cases of broken legs it is better to kill the bird at once.

Birds have a weak place in their back, a little lower down than the hump, which sometimes gets broken whilst fighting, or by other means ; these then lose the use of their legs, whilst they continue to feed well and in other ways appear all right, but of course, they eventually die.

Birds will often get a piece of bone stuck in the throat, generally one of the joints of the backbone of a sheep or goat. It can often be forced back and taken out of the mouth again; but sometimes a sharp point will penetrate the flesh, and it cannot be moved either way; then an incision must be made in the throat (carefully avoiding the comparatively hard wind-pipe, which can easily be felt), and the bone taken out. Before making the incision, the skin should be drawn on one side, so that after the operation the incisions in the skin and in the flesh come in different places ; this, when the skin is sewn together, greatly assists the excluding of the air from the wound, and its consequently rapid healing. There is no danger in the operation if done carefully. Of broken wings we have treated in the chapter on " The Ostrich."

# CHAPTER XXV.

## ECONOMY AND CREDIT.

WITHOUT the first the farmer will not long have the second. Given the first, he will be exceedingly careful how he avails himself of the second. Economy and saving, in all walks of life, should be practised if a man does not want to run the risk of some day finding himself in money difficulties. But whilst the professional man or merchant may live up to his income in early years, and, by increased connection and consequent extended business, eventually make a fortune, the farmer has no other way of increasing his income than by saving, and thereby adding to his stock-in-trade. The Ostrich-farmer who lives up to his income is simply waiting for the first great drought, outbreak of disease in his stock, or other untoward event, to begin descending the ladder and eventually to become bankrupt.

It is impossible to impress too strongly on the young farmer the importance of economy, not only in his own personal expenditure, but in every item that would come under the category of what I have termed "dead capital"—that is, everything that does not produce something saleable. A horse is dead capital: it does not multiply, nor yet produce anything, and yet how many more horses most young farmers keep than they need! It will take £22 to buy anything of a horse; the same money will buy a nice "feather" bird, which will give at least £12 a year in feathers. The bird is not more likely to die than the horse, and they will both cost him about equal in keeping. In three years the horse will have decreased, say £5, in value; the bird will have increased £20. So that, after three years, the gain to the young farmer, by having sold the horse and bought another bird with the money, will be £61. The same thing runs all through. One man takes two spans of oxen to manage a large farm, while another gets along equally well with only one, and in their place has a dozen cows, giving a dozen calves and a lot of butter every year; whilst the other man's extra oxen are decreasing in value.

This is one of the main reasons why those who commence with a considerable capital so invariably lose it. They will not study economy, or else they rush to the other extreme; and whilst they are lavish in their private expenditure, are so stingy about their farm expenditure that they let their birds die for want of feeding; they will not put up good sound fences, and consequently their men's time is half taken up looking for lost birds, and their birds break their legs in badly-erected fences; they do not provide proper housing for the chicks in bad weather, and consequently lose a lot now and again; or they do not keep enough men for the work there is to do, and insufficiently pay and feed those they have, and consequently never have a good labourer. It is to steer the middle course that we must have experience.

The man who begins with lavish careless expenditure, who is quoted as such an open-handed fellow, and who is only too ready to endorse a friend's bill, will end generally as a mean miser; whilst the man who is economical, punctual in his payments, not in too great a hurry to lend his purse, and that nothing would induce to sign a promissory note without value received, but who is both just and generous to all about him, will in the long run do far the most to help on his fellow-men.

Credit for short dates is but too easily obtained, nearly every auction sale being held subject to three months' credit on a promissory note, subject to an endorser if required. The birds on the "halves" system is also a credit system, but one in which the borrower pays a terribly long interest. The purchase of land is always on credit of payments by instalments extending over to two or three years, but generally subject to two sureties; or, if not, about a third is generally required in cash, when the remainder can mostly be raised on a mortgage. The banks very rarely give the farmer credit, excepting in the form of discounting bills bearing two approved names. Credit may be obtained, too, on a preferent bond; but, as this is fatal to further credit, it is only resorted to by a man on the verge of bankruptcy, or where a young man is being started in farming by a relative, or by other people's money, and the bond is given to provide for the lender getting paid in preference to others. In this latter way it is a perfectly reasonable means of obtaining credit. The only other means of credit available for the farmer is for goods supplied by the merchant with whom he deals, and which are usually supplied on a six months' credit, and this will even be allowed to run to twelve months or more, bearing interest at six or eight per cent. per annum; but when over six months is given, the amount is generally covered by a promissory note payable on demand or at a fixed date.

This latter is extensively used, and Juvenis when he first starts may be compelled to use it; but the sooner he can do without it, and adopt cash or monthly payments, the better. He will then get five per cent. discount on his purchases; whereas if he ran a half-yearly account, the goods being purchased at all times in the half-year, he would only average a three months' credit all round. So that by paying cash he makes twenty per cent. per annum on the amount of his quarterly purchases.

To Juvenis and others, the merchant keeping his carriage and living in style may appear a wealthy man; and as he is very accommodating—as it is his business to be, as long as he knows Juvenis has the means to pay—Juvenis is very apt to think it does not matter if his account is large and has been long accumulating. But woe to him if a commercial crisis comes, and he suddenly finds the merchant insolvent, and he is called upon by the creditors to pay up sharp.

Juvenis should on no account ever sell his produce on credit. Produce is cash all the world over, and reasonably so, as the merchant, although he may not have the balance at his bank to pay for it, can always go there and raise the wind on the produce.

Juvenis will find that in selling his surplus increase, or other stock, he will generally have to give credit; but, as a rule, he should not give more than three months, and had certainly much better decline to sell to a customer of whose stability he has any doubts, than run the risk of not being paid; and he must, on no account, let any terms of friendship or acquaintanceship he may be on with the would-be purchaser influence him. Directly it comes to buying and selling, neither party has the slightest right to think of that: for both parties' sake, and for their future friendship, let it be business, hard business.

Juvenis will do well to remember the old saying: "There is no charity in business, and no business in charity." When he is well to do, he may soften the first part as much as he likes.

Juvenis can always get rid of the risks of bad bills by selling his stock through an auctioneer, when he will either take his bill, for which he will be charged five per cent. over and above the government dues, or he can arrange to be paid in cash, when he will have to submit to a gross deduction on the vendor's roll of from eight to ten per cent., but this he will find out-and-out a better plan than taking a bill of which he has the slightest doubt.

There is no reason why Juvenis, if he has no debts, and has a plucking of feathers, that after allowing for casualties would be sold in three months, should not buy more stock on credit; but if he is wise he will wait, and then, with cash in hand, in nine cases out of ten, he will buy at a price that will more than compensate him for the three months' loss of profit.

Juvenis should never be led into buying what he does not want, merely because it is cheap, or, as he will constantly hear fellows saying, "to do a spec." He

M

may see wealthy men who do nothing but what would appear to him to be speculating. He must not be misled : these men do not speculate : they are stock-dealers, *alias* middlemen, who, if successful, work as hard at their business as any farmer, have generally a great knowledge of the country and of every man's affairs in their district, are excellent judges of stock, and in the great majority of cases know before they buy where they can sell again, even if they are not. as is often the case, buying on commission.    But even if they do buy on spec, they have command of money, and it is immaterial to them whether they wait one or two years for a sale, provided they can eventually make a corresponding profit.    But not so Juvenis, who, perhaps at a sale, hearing people exclaim, " How cheap !—by Jove, there is money to be made on these ! " gets tempted, and buys on credit.    He gets the stock home, and tells all his neighbours what a spec he has made.    They come and look at them ; all agree how cheap, but somehow do not buy.    " Never mind," thinks Juvenis, " there's Mr. B., of H—.    I will go over and see him.    I know he wants some of this kind of stock ;" but, strange to say, when he gets to H., he finds B. bought what he wanted only a few days ago, and, stranger still, at even a lower figure than Juvenis gave ; and in the course of conversation B. says, "If I were you, I would sell those things sharp. I don't quite like the looks of things ; people are throwing birds in the market in all directions, and I heard that up in the Karoo the drought is so bad, that they are letting them go for a mere song." Juvenis is now beginning heartily to wish he had never given that nod to the auctioneer that made him the possessor of these birds. The three months' credit he got has nearly run out, and he sees nothing for it but to ask the auctioneer to renew the bill. To this the auctioneer probably consents, after some demur, but insists on £100 of it being paid. Juvenis is now driven to going to his merchant, and getting an advance of this amount on his next plucking. The merchant looks grave, tells him that the late fall in feathers is much heavier than the papers admitted, that his private advices from London are that they are likely to go even lower in the next few months ; but he knows Juvenis's word can be relied on, and writes him the necessary cheque.

Juvenis now begins to see that it was no slip of Mr. W.'s and Mr. S.'s, the two dealers at the sale, that they did not buy. In fact, if he had only known it, those men had hardly bought a head of stock for themselves for months past. They had long since seen an unsteadiness in the commercial barometer. The last bank statements had shown them much, numbers of

M 2

their customers coming for renewals had shown them more, and conversations with auctioneers and others in business had convinced them that one of those terribly depressed times was coming; caused by what? perhaps nobody can tell, but to which all the colonies are subject; times when property of every description will fall perhaps fifty per cent. and be hardly saleable at that ; perhaps lasting only a few months, and succeeded by a rapid rise to even higher prices than ever; perhaps lasting years, and followed by a very gradual rise ;— a time when those that have been laughed at as slow-going and cautious in the good times, are investing their savings in buying up insolvent estates at prices that will some day prove a fortune. A time when those who in the good times have been the admired and envied ones for their dash and speculative turn, are going crash in all directions.

Juvenis does not yet see all this, but he sees that his speculation is becoming a serious matter. He had as many birds as his farm, his staff, and his plant would manage, and he cannot attend to these extra birds properly ; already some have got lost, the others have fallen off in condition, and some have even died, more or less of poverty. At last he makes up his mind to sell them by auction, and is right glad to be rid of them, at a loss of thirty per cent. and all his trouble.

Let us hope he will have learnt that a man cannot really succeed at more than one thing at a time ; that an Ostrich-farmer's business is to make his birds and his cattle increase, and produce the greatest quantity and best quality of feathers possible, and that even if he is successful with a few speculations, he will have lost quite as much by their interference with his proper business as he made. That if he takes money wanted in his proper business to speculate with, it will inevitably be attended with loss; whilst if he does it on credit, sooner or later his experience will be that of Juvenis.

As we have seen in former chapters, unless Juvenis's capital fund to invest at starting was counted in thousands, he will at first be obliged to use credit in some form, even on a hired farm, and consequently a considerable portion of his earnings will go to the capitalist ; but if he is strictly economical and fairly successful, a few years will see him out of debt, and the whole stock his own; but by this time his lease will probably be nearly expired, and his landlord will not re-let, or if he will re-let, will not make the improvements which Juvenis feels he cannot do without. His stock is now so large that he cannot do without more fencing, he has already got as much bush fencing as he can keep in repair; wire or stone wall means sinking capital on another man's property ; besides, his breeding birds are so many that he must have better buildings for his chicks.

He has now reached the second great critical time in his affairs : if he can carry himself successfully over it, he is a made man. On the one hand, to track to another farm will throw his stock back, and in every way cause him serious loss ; on the other, to purchase the farm he is on will cause him to incur a very heavy liability ; but if the owner will sell at anything like a reasonable figure, and give him extended credit, with very little to be paid down, this is his wisest course ; if the owner will not sell, he should endeavour to get a suitable farm on a short lease, with right of purchase at a fixed price and fixed terms of payment. In either case he is then in a position to make what improvements are absolutely necessary for the well-being of his stock, but in this he must use the utmost discretion and economy. His position financially is not nearly equal to what it was as a tenant, the transfer dues and first instalment will have walked off with his spare cash, the interest on the unpaid portions will probably be more than what he paid as a rental, and he has the portions of the purchase-money to meet every six months.

Let him not be too sanguine ; let him bear in mind the chances of change in the commercial barometer ; let him turn over every shilling two or three times before he spends it; let him bear in mind that if he cannot meet the instalments as they become due he will be in the power of another; that this other may have been compelled to discount the bills Juvenis gave, and that unless he can meet them, there is great danger of all his former years of toil being swept away; for he is then not in the hands of one willing to be forbearing and to help him, but in the hands of some bank or other company, and "Companies have no souls," as Juvenis will quickly find out, and at which he must not be surprised: the directors' duty is to see that no unnecessary risk is run with the shareholders' money.

Not till two-thirds, or, at least, a half, of the purchase money is paid off can Juvenis breathe freely, or consider that he is financially out of danger, for this is all that he can ordinarily trust to being able to raise on a mortgage bond in the open market. But as long as he has a mortgage bond of any sort on his property, he should not incur other liabilities for the sake of improving his property. Whilst it may be a question with him as funds come in whether it is better to improve or to get rid of the mortgage, this will entirely depend upon the returns the proposed improvements are likely to give.

Another mistake that is often made is this—a man

gets a sort of earth-mania, and buys farm upon farm, only paying off a little on each; even a rich man thus soon becomes embarrassed, and if a commercial crisis comes will be utterly ruined.

But a far commoner mistake is this: a man has got up as far as where we have just left Juvenis, with no debts except a moderate mortgage; when an adjacent property comes into the market—one that would make a most desirable addition to his property—and he is tempted; the owner would probably accept a second mortgage bond on the other property as sufficient collateral security; the chance, he thinks, may never occur again in his lifetime, &c. But let him steadfastly resist the temptation. True, the chance may never occur again, but if he waits till he is in a better position he will be surprised how many equally tempting things will turn up, and if he purchases now he puts himself in quite as dangerous a position as. he was in when he firs purchased land. Besides which, he will not be able to stock it; and if he lets it, it will in all probability not bring him in the interest on the purchase money.

It will be seen that there are only two periods in a farmer's career when he should avail himself to any considerable extent of credit: the first, when he first starts: the second, when he buys his farm. His whole business is essentially different to that of the merchant, who safely can, and most probably does, avail himself to a large extent of credit throughout his career. The merchant's goods are—thanks to insurances—not liable to destruction as far as he is concerned. He has two dangers only to apprehend : that of the inability of his customers to pay him, and of a fall in produce. But the farmer is much more affected by a fall in produce, as it lowers the value of his whole stock, which is, besides, subject at all times to be decimated by diseases, droughts, floods, and even possibly total destruction by some murrain. Consequently, he cannot insure his stock ; could he do so, he might safely avail himself of credit to a large extent. Directly he ceases to be merely a farmer by becoming a land-owner as well, he finds the means, as the merchant does, of using credit on all sides of him. Why? Because that part of his capital which is invested in land is to a great extent perfectly safe.

# CHAPTER XXVI.

## DESTRUCTION OF CARNIVOROUS ANIMALS.

CLOSELY connected with the subject of fencing is that of the destruction of carnivorous animals, especially in a country like this which so abounds with every species of them. The lion is only found so far in the interior now that it need not be remarked upon; and, strange to say, the wild dogs which are so destructive to sheep and goats when running at large, have not yet learnt to destroy our Ostriches, but they may do so any day. The worst of the carnivora to the Ostrich-farmer is, *par excellence*, the tiger; next, the jackal, the wild cat for little chicks, the lynx for larger ones, and the natives' and other people's dogs worse than any of these.

A thousand years ago the then civilised world was enlightened enough to offer large rewards for the destruction of carnivora, and even sixty years ago we did so at the Cape; but the ordinance has been allowed to fall in abeyance; and an enlightened (?), responsible Ministry replied to the author in a letter he addressed to them on the subject, "they did not consider it was a matter which concerned them." So that we must not

BIRD WITH NEST.

be surprised that the tiger and the jackal are as numerous in the country as they were twenty years ago.

The tiger will often live for a long time in close proximity to an Ostrich-camp without molesting the birds ; but once let him—or rather I should say she, as it is generally the vixen that is the offending party— kill a bird, and the farmer will have no peace till the tiger is killed.    If the bird or animal which was killed the previous night is found, and strychnine put in without moving the carcase in any way, the tiger will often return, and be found poisoned not far off.    Pills—that is, lumps of meat with about a grain of strychnine— should also be laid about in all directions ; whilst a bush fence across the kloof, with holes left for the tiger to creep through should be made—in each of which should be placed one of the ordinary double-spring tiger gins that are sold in all colonial towns.    Or, a little half-moon bush hockey should be made, and a sheep or goat tied up in it, with either spring guns or gins across the entrance.    But the farmer who would save himself from further heavy losses should relax no efforts until he is rid of his enemy.

Jackals are very destructive to young birds.    They cannot kill an old bird, but are very apt to frighten them at night, and the farmer should always poison them off.    This is easily done by laying a few hundred

pills about, especially on the roads and little foot-
tracks ; or, better still, by dragging a paunch or part of
a dead carcase across the veldt at sundown, occasionally
dropping a pill on the line of scent.   The farmer, if he
notices, will soon discover on his farm the warrens of
holes that the jackals inhabit, generally not more than
one or two on a farm ; and when he has once got them
reduced down, should he again hear one barking, he
has only to lay pills at the warren to at once destroy
it.    Many farmers are frightened to lay pills in
their Ostrich-camps, but they need not be afraid.   We
have made it an invariable practice to do so, and unless
the birds have been trained to eat meat they will not
touch them.

Wild cats are exceedingly numerous, and very
destructive to the chicks when they first hatch in the
veldt.   The only safeguard is to destroy them with
poison ; and if the camp abuts on to a river, or there is
much bush about, it is always advisable to lay poison
some days before the brood is expected out.

The lynx is not a common animal, but is very bold
and destructive when he does come ; but he is not
capable of attacking chicks over four months old.
He, too, must be settled with poison.

An Ostrich-farmer should never permit a native to
keep a dog, and better still if he does not keep one

himself. Where there are dogs there will always be accidents. Even if the dogs do not chase the birds—which the quietest dogs cannot be perfectly trusted not to do at some time or other, the birds will " scrik " from them at night, and many are thus killed or injured. We have not seen that birds brought up amongst dogs are less frightened at them than those which have not been, though most farmers suppose that they are so.

Monkeys will sometimes bother with the chicks in the veldt. They catch them and play with them, and often end by knocking out their eyes. The best plan is to shoot a few of the monkeys, when the rest will leave the locality.

The Ostrich-farmer should bear in mind that strychnine used *ad libitum* is one of his best friends.

# CHAPTER XXVII.

## LAND LAWS.

THE tenure under which the land in the Cape Colony has passed from the possession of the Crown into the hands of private individuals, and the laws under which, at the present time, private individuals can become possessed of Crown lands, and under what reservations, is a matter of primary interest to everybody in the country, but especially so to the farmer. We shall now, therefore, give a short sketch of the manner in which the Crown became possessed of the land, and then dispossessed itself in favour of private individuals, under certain reservations, together with the laws at present in force for providing for such transfer.

In 1652 the first settlement in South Africa was founded at Table Bay, on the present site of Cape Town, by the Dutch East India Company, for victualling their ships. As time went on they continued to allow the Company's discharged servants and others to occupy patches of land, upon the payment of a small annual rental of £4 16s., called "Quitrent," and these patches were known as "loan places." As the community spread farther inland, and stock-raising became the main industry of the people, the size of these places came to be about 3,000 morgen, or a little over 6,000 acres, which is recognised at the present day as the size of a full farm. This went on and on, the boundaries of the colony always extending north and east. In 1813, seven years after the final establishment of the British Government in the colony, and the boundary eastward had been fixed at the Great Fish River, Governor Sir John Cradock invited all possessors of " loan places " to submit their claims and receive title-deeds for the land, to be known under the name of " Perpetual Quitrent Tenure." Previous to this (and even since), small portions of land had been granted as " Freehold," but the great mass of the land is held under the above-mentioned " Quitrent Tenure," which only differs from " Freehold " in that the Government reserve their rights to precious stones, gold and silver, and the right of making and repairing roads, and of taking materials for that purpose without compensating the owner, together with the perpetual annual payment of £4 16s. In lands granted under this tenure, subsequent to this date, the reservation was made that " no slaves should be employed on the land," and that " the land should be brought into such a state of cultivation as it was capable of ;" the first of these conditions ceased to have any meaning after the abolition of slavery in 1834 ; the other condition has never been enforced, and has become obsolete.

Up to the year 1860, the governor had the power of granting lands under Perpetual Quitrent tenure to whom he thought fit. Most of the land in British Kaffraria and Queenstown, taken from the Kaffirs at the end of the wars of 1846 and 1850, was granted to those who had borne arms, with the further servitude on them of personal occupation and liability to military service ; but these last conditions were abolished by act of the colonial parliament in 1868.

In 1860 the first act was passed which took the power out of the hands of the governor, and provided that all Crown lands should be submitted to public auction before they could be alienated. A quitrent, equal to one per cent. of the supposed value was retained, but the tenure was in most cases better than that of the old quitrent farms : because the government was bound to compensate the owner for all land it re-took from him for roads, railways, or other public purposes; whilst the reservation of precious minerals and stones was seldom inserted, and the quitrent was redeemable by the payment of fifteen years' purchase. When the Crown land lay contiguous to private property, the divisional councils had the power of fixing the value, and title could be obtained without its being first submitted to public auction. But this act is no longer in force as regards any further alienation of land from the Crown.

In 1864 an act was passed enabling the government to lease Crown lands for twenty-one years ; which leases by a subsequent act, No. 5, of 1870, could be converted into real property on " Quitrent Tenure," at such price as should be fixed by arbitration. In no case could the arbitrators fix on a less sum than what the yearly rental capitalised at six per cent. would come to ; or, in round numbers, sixteen times the rental. A perpetual annual quitrent of one per cent. on this amount was also imposed.

These two acts continued in force until 1878, when they were repealed in so far as any lands not disposed of up to that date were concerned. But a large extent of country was taken up under the act of 1864, and although in many cases the lessees took the land at rentals exceeding its value, owing to the spurt which Ostrich-farming has now given to the value of land, these farms will probably before the expiration of the twenty-one years' lease be converted under the provision of the act No. 5 of 1870 into quitrent farms.

In 1870 and 1877 two acts were passed which dealt with the disposal to agriculturists of small farms not exceeding 500 acres in extent, and which will be

N

more fully noticed hereafter ; with these two exceptions
we have now seen how and under what conditions the
whole of the Crown lands passed into the hands of
private persons up to the year 1878, in which year
an act was passed repealing all former land acts, excepting No. 4 of 1870, No. 5 of 1870, and No. 10 of 1877.

This act—No. 14 of 1878—is undoubtedly the most
perfect act for dealing with Crown lands that has ever
been passed in any British colony.   The great danger that
all colonies have struggled against is that of their Crown
lands getting into the hands of large speculators, instead
of into the hands of men who would live upon them
and draw out their latent wealth.   This act, whilst
giving the farmer a perfect title to his land, and thereby
holding out to him every inducement to build upon
it and improve it, only requires him to pay down
surveying expenses and one year's rental : thus allowing a man of very small means to enjoy all the privi-
leges and advantages of a landed proprietor, and
enabling him, if successful in after-years, to get rid of
his annual payment by paying down twenty years'
rental, which frees the land from any further quitrent.
The severe competition which has thus been brought
about ensures the Crown lands fetching their full value,
and puts an effectual stop to the danger of the land
getting into the hands of a few wealthy men.

In the colony proper the Crown lands which have not been alienated consist mainly, as might be supposed, of land destitute of permanent water, or covered with scrub, or precipitous hills, or that are in some way inferior to the other lands, and have consequently been neglected by settlers. But as a very large extent of beautiful country has lately been taken from the native tribes that have rebelled, the whole of which will be sold either in small lots to agriculturists under the acts of 1870 and 1877, or in large blocks of about 6,000 acres under the act of 1878, we think it advisable to epitomise some of the leading features of the acts of 1878 and 1877, the latter of which embraces all the features of that of 1870, whilst making the act applicable to assisted immigrants, and the payments somewhat easier.

The Crown Lands Act of 1878 provides "that all waste and unappropriated Crown lands in the colony shall, except as is hereinafter excepted, be disposed of on perpetual quitrent for the highest annual rent that can be obtained for the same by public auction."

"That the auction shall take place at the Civil Commissioner's office of the division in which the land is situated."

"That three months' notice of such sale shall be given in the Government Gazette and in some local

N 2

newspaper, such notice to state the minimum rent that will be accepted."

" First year's rent to be paid in advance, and sureties given for the next two, or, in lieu of such sureties, two years' rent to be paid in advance."

" The rent can at any time be capitalised by the payment of twenty times the amount, or portions of not less than one quarter at a time can be so capitalised."

" The expenses of survey, erection of beacons, and of the title-deeds, to be paid at any time the government may fix."

" The nature of the tenure to be known as ' Perpetual Quitrent,' and subject to a special servitude that may be stated in the conditions of sale ; as also all roads marked on the diagram to remain open, unless closed as by law is provided. Government has the right to resume possession of part or the whole for public purposes on compensating the owner, and reserves deposits of gold, silver, or precious stones."

" All lands not disposed of under this Act to be leased for any term not exceeding three years."

" The exceptions are, agricultural lands disposed of under the acts of 1870 and 1877, and where a piece of Crown land adjoins that of private owners ; when, after certain due formalities have been gone through, the government may dispose of such piece of land privately to the adjoining owner or owners at such quitrent as the governor shall decide, or as shall be decided upon by three arbitrators."

The Agricultural Immigrants' Land Act, being No. 16 of 1877, provides " that the governor may from time to time set aside suitable areas for disposal under this act ; the immigrant not to be allowed to lease more than 500 acres, the term to be for ten years, at the rate of 1s. per acre per annum."

" The rent to be payable on the *expiration* of each year."

" The lessee is bound to erect on the land a dwelling-house of the value of £20 before the expiration of two years, and afterwards to cultivate one acre out of every ten."

" After the tenth annual payment, and the expenses of survey and title, he receives a grant on perpetual quit-rent tenure, subject to an annual quitrent of 1 per cent. on the ten years' rental."

" He can on allotment pay the whole ten years' rent down, or at any time subsequently the remaining portion, and receive title at once, but he cannot sell the grant till after the expiration of five years from its first allotment."

" On failure of the lessee complying with any of the above conditions, the government can declare such lease to be forfeited, when it shall be put up to public auction, but any surplus accruing from the sale goes to the first lessee."

Such are the three acts under which all Crown lands are now disposed of, and it must be owned that for liberality of terms they are not to be beaten by any colony under the Crown. Even the agricultural immigrant, if he possesses the means to purchase one or two pairs of birds, or a few young birds, together with his agriculture, would be in a fair way to a competency, even if not to a fortune.

With the quieting-down of the native wars that have done so much harm to South Africa, and those which are now raging, which ought never to have occurred— and would not have done so had the present government only listened to the voice of those who, having the true welfare of the country at heart, and knowing the natives, tried their utmost to dissuade the government from continuing their mad, headstrong policy of indiscriminate disarmament which has brought all the present troubles upon the Cape Colony. The bitter experience which the country has now had will induce in the future such a keen interest in politics that such madness is not likely again to occur.

To say more on this subject would be to trench' on the domain of politics, which would be foreign to the present work; but we say so much to induce the intending immigrant or others to look into the matter, and not jump to the conclusion, as they naturally might, that South Africa will always be in a state of warfare.

To conclude : let it be borne in mind by all intending to emigrate from England that the colony has now on its hands a large amount of as fine lands as might be wished for. That the only drawback to these is their contiguity to native tribes ; but this contiguity gives a counter-advantage, viz., that of cheap labour. That these lands will be disposed of partially in agricultural blocks, not exceeding 500 acres in extent, and all that like to apply for them will be able to do so under the provisions of Act No. 4 of 1870, or, in the case of " Assisted Immigrants," under the still more favourable conditions, as regards payment, of Act No. 10 of 1877.

The remainder will be disposed of in blocks of from 4,000 to 6,000 acres, under the provisions of Act No. 14 of 1878.

The name "Assisted Immigrant" applies to those who are sent out to the colony at the expense of the Cape government.

# CHAPTER XXVIII.

## HORSES AND CATTLE.

Every Ostrich-farmer must keep some horses. The number, of course, will depend upon the number of birds he has. Birds are always apt to get astray, and unless followed up as soon as missed, they may go long distances, even if they are not altogether lost. It is much cheaper, quicker, and more effectual to send men on horseback than to send them on foot, when they will probably not go half far enough, spending much of their time asleep under a bush. And much of the feeding can be done by a man on horseback, with a led horse carrying a pack-saddle. Pack-saddles are not half so much used in the country as they might be; they can be bought in the colony, with breeching and breastplate, and complete, excepting the side bags, for £4, and the bags can be made on the farm out of sacks.

The farmer should never give a long price for his horses—what he wants are quiet mokes, the quieter the better for working with birds. Their food should not cost him anything, as he should let them run in one of his camps, but he must have a stable or warm shed to put them in at night, when the horse-sickness makes its appearance. This horse-sickness is the only thing he need much dread : it generally breaks out once in five years. It begins in December or January, mildly at first, but increasing in virulence, and disappears after the first few frosts in June. Although the exact cause is unknown, there can be no doubt it is connected with malaria in the night air : as, if during its prevalence, a horse is stabled from shortly before sundown until the dew is off the grass in the morning, it will never contract the disease ; and where this cannot be done, keeping a nose-bag on all night is a great preventive ; whilst even putting them in a kraal with a lot of other stock is good.

The first symptoms noticeable are, that the horse suddenly breathes heavily, droops its ears, and makes for its stable. Froth generally comes from its nostrils, and in twenty-four hours it dies. It is not in the slightest degree infections or contagious, but in a season when the disease is bad, a single night's exposure, when the dew is falling heavily and there is a cold clammy feel in the atmosphere, will be fatal to a large per-centage of the horses that are at large, especially if feeding in a valley. Some people imagine that the cobwebs on the grass have something to do with it, but this is only owing to the cobwebs showing out very distinctly in the morning after these dewy nights. The post-mortem examinations show violent inflammation of the lungs, but beyond this the whole disease is wrapped in mystery. The better condition the animal is in, and the less work it does, the more liable it is to take the disease; and we remember seeing a veterinary surgeon, who was holding forth very dogmatically that it was nothing but over-riding and bad treatment, being completely posed by being asked how he accounted for unbroken animals being more subject to it than working animals. A remarkable feature is that a sucking foal never contracts it, whilst it is said that if a dog eats the entrails of one that has died of this disease, it will kill it. There is no known cure, but a few recover, after which they are said never to be again subject to the disease. In the high parts of the colony, and on the tops of mountains, the disease is unknown, and these are the parts where most of the horses are bred. To attempt breeding them in low lands sooner or later ends in loss.

Glanders are often very prevalent, and directly the farmer sees it in a horse he should shoot him; but he must not mistake the much more common disease, strangles, for it. With strangles a horse only wants to be put in a camp, and rested for a month or two, to be cured. If worked he will infect other horses, and the disease will be very apt to run on into glanders. With these exceptions a farmer's horses running at grass will be but little troubled with disease. The principal things that will bother him will be horses getting lame and bad sore backs ; and for these, turning them out for a spell is the cheapest and best remedy. When travelling, if the horse is saddled off every two hours, even if only for a few minutes, to allow him to stale, and is not allowed to drink water whilst hot, he will seldom hurt in South Africa. If a chafe is seen, raw brandy should be put on it *ad libitum* to harden the flesh. If the horse gets an attack of gripes, a good and easily procured remedy is a soda-water bottle of gin with a wine-glassful of pepper in it.

The farmer should look well to his saddles, as one badly-stuffed saddle will soon lay up several horses.

Cattle are an essential item on every Ostrich-farm : not only working oxen, but cows, to supply fresh milk and butter to the farmer, and thick milk to the native servants. Even with a few head of cows, the butter he can make and sell in the nearest town will pay all the expenses attending them; whilst the food they supply, for native servants, in the shape of thick milk, together with their increase, gives a very handsome profit. Excepting on the coast and some portions of the grass veldt, 90 to 100 per cent. of the calves will be reared with no further trouble than seeing that the herd does not take too much milk from the mothers, and that the calves never by any chance get to the mothers in the veldt, thus getting a sudden bellyful of milk, which is often the cause of scour and death. If kept too much in the hock—especially if it is small, and has been long in use—the calves get lousy, lick themselves, swallow a lot of hair, which sets up violent indigestion, and from which many succumb. The louse can be cured by washings of tobacco-water, or other vermifuges; but the preventative should be sought in letting the calves run day and night, and having a new and clean calf-hock. Where practicable, there is nothing like having the cattle kraal in the fence of an enclosure; so that the cows go out one side of the fence, and the calves the other. By this means, excepting on the coast lands, nearly all will be reared. But on the coast lands, in spite of every care, probably not 10 per cent. of the calves are reared. The only successful way there seems to be is, never to let them out to graze until they are twelve months old.

In Natal, red water is very fatal; but this disease is not known in the Cape Colony, where the three main diseases are lung-sickness (pleuro-pneumonia), gall-sickness, and spon-sickness (quarter evil). Lung-sickness is the great bugbear with cattle, as from its terribly communicative nature the farmer never feels safe. His best course, directly he sees it, is to shoot the infected beast, and to continue to do so whenever it again re-appears; then it is an open question whether it is advisable to inoculate or not. But, whatever he does, he should never let an infected beast live, as for every one that he cures he probably infects several. A farmer with a troop of cattle, if he buys others, should always put them in a camp by themselves for at least three months before he allows them to mix with his own.

Gall-sickness is the next most serious disease. It is purely a disease of the liver and of the digestive organs, and is, of course, in no way infectious. In all cases where sweet veldt cattle are brought on to sour veldt, a considerable per-centage suffer. The best and most simple remedy is a quart of linseed oil with a wine-glass of turpentine for a full-grown beast, and half the amount for a young beast. Failing linseed oil, from one to two pounds of Epsom salts can be used instead. Having given the dose, leave the beast alone; much harm is often done by the farmer getting im-patient at the apparently slow working of the medicine, and giving another dose on the top of it. In all cases of physicking, having made up your mind what is best medicine to be given, give it, and leave the rest to nature and perfect rest. With gall-sickness, once let a beast recover so far as to get up and nibble, and it may be considered out of danger. The surest indication of this disease is a swelling above and round the eyes.

Spon-sickness : this, or some disease closely resembling it, has always been very fatal with young stock on the coast-lands, but of late years it has made its appearance in a virulent form on some farms on the veldt, between the hard Karoo and the sour veldt. It is in no way infectious; but if one beast dies of it the farmer must take alarm, as the same causes will have been at work with the whole of them. It is essentially an inflammatory fever, and is only seen in stock that are in good condition, or those that are running rapidly into condition. The great thing is to reduce them down by kraaling them at night, and keeping them in till late in the morning; and a seton made of rough tow, and dipped in turpentine, cantharides, or some other irritant, can be inserted in the dewlap, and occasionally pulled to keep up an irritation. If a beast is once affected, a cure is very doubtful, but purgatives and bleeding are the right treatment.

Tape-worm, even in full-grown cattle, has been getting somewhat common of late. It is known, as with the Ostrich, by the segments being seen on the dung. It can be cured by giving 3 ozs. of turpentine in milk upon an empty stomach, and should certainly be got rid of as soon as seen, to prevent it spreading.

The young farmer when commencing should buy fairly good cows, and always keep a moderately well-bred colonial-born bull, with a good dash of English or Friesland blood. The more imported blood in the progeny, the higher price they will fetch; but if too well-bred, they will not breed so freely, and suffer terribly in our severe droughts. Once having got them too well-bred, if an attempt is made to bring them back by introducing common bulls, the result is generally horrid, ill-made mongrels, possessing all the bad qualities of both breeds.

As the towns grow large, and artificial food is grown for feeding the milk-cows, the importance of having breeds that give a great quantity of milk will be felt, as then the dairyman will find it to his advantage to give treble the price for a cow that will give three times the quantity of milk that a common cow will. The value of the calves will be a minor consideration, whilst the small number he will have to feed will be of primary consideration. But until artificial food is grown for them it is useless to get a cow with great milk-producing powers. To the farmer, rapid increase and a constitution that can stand vicissitudes, is of more importance than large milk-producing qualities.

The importing of pure stock and raising thorough-bred cattle is essentially a rich man's business, as he can afford to lose several imported animals if he can eventually attain his end, whilst the not getting an immediate return for his investment is of no importance to him; but not so with the poorer man, who, if he loses an imported bull, probably cannot afford to replace him, and he loses nearly all the advantage he would have got if he could have afforded to keep on; whilst even if he is lucky the return is too distant to suit him, and the risks are very great. These remarks apply equally to Ostriches and other stock. The new beginner, whilst avoiding inferior birds, should not be led into giving fancy prices for what are said to be extraordinarily superior birds.

# CHAPTER XXIX.

THE next great difficulty to the constant and ever-recurring droughts, is the uncertain supply and inferior quality of the labour attainable ; and as a young man might even have had an apprenticeship of a few years on a farm where the master had the knack of getting on with his labourers, and during a time when labourers happened to be extra plentiful, he might even be deceived, and not calculate this difficulty at its true weight; so that we need not offer any apology for a few remarks on this subject.

The great bulk of the work on a farm is and will continue to be done by natives, and how to manage them successfully can only be learnt from experience. All extra work on a farm requiring mechanical skill, such as fencing, is nearly always done by the assistants on the farm, or by white labourers, who can generally be procured by enquiries amongst the neighbours or by advertising in a local paper, though not always just when they are wanted. Much heavy work, such as dam-making, is often done by white navvies,

o

but the everyday work, such as herding and feeding birds, wagon-driving, ploughing, &c., is all done by natives. And half the success or non-success of the Ostrich-farmer will depend upon whether he has the knack of managing them, coupled with personal industry.

To obtain this knack, a man must possess all the qualities that are requisite to command white men : he must be firm but not tyrannous, he must show a kindly interest in their welfare whilst avoiding any familiarity, or any unnecessary messing and muddling with them. He must be strictly just, and more ready to defraud himself than to exact the last penny on any doubtful point. He must be liberal in wages and rations, and not too ready to find fault, ever remembering how much that he does—and that he thinks he does so perfectly—would be found fault with if he had a master over him. He should strive to the utmost to be the same every day, and never give way to peevish temper ; though a good, wholesome reprimand occasionally, and letting them see you are not to be trifled with, is sometimes necessary. These are the qualities that go to make a successful commander of men in other parts of the world ; whilst at the Cape a man must have over and above these a special aptitude for managing the different natives he has to do with ; as the Hottentot, the Fingo, and the Kaffir, all have different peculiarities of character which he must study. They will all be hired as general monthly servants, but for all this he should study each man, and strive as much as possible to give him the work he likes best. Some like herding, whilst others would sooner take 10s. a month to do general work than 30s. to herd. Some men cannot bear to see their wives employed in the house or at other work, whilst others are delighted to do so. Some men will be exceedingly good servants as long as they are on the farm, whilst if you send them to town with the wagon, or on an errand, you might as well try to stop an avalanche as to stop them from getting drunk. Some men will willingly let their big boys work, and these often make better herds for birds than the men; but when the farmer employs them he should never let anything induce him to flog them: he should always send for the father and let him do it; he will give them twice the licking that the master ever would, and it takes far more effect on the boy than the master doing it; whilst if the master does it, the father will generally give notice to leave, or object to the boy working any more.

Sometimes a native servant will goad and annoy a master till human nature can stand no more, and he " goes for him; " but in nine cases out of ten he makes

o 2

a mistake by doing so, as the man is generally a worthless character that no amount of thrashing will ever improve, and is one the master had much better be rid of, and whose summary dismissal would have a good effect upon the others; whilst by thrashing him the master is very apt to get a bad name, and the others inwardly resent it, though they may not show it. The only occasion on which a master should ever thrash a native servant is when he is thoroughly insolent; but if a master guards his own conduct carefully, such occasions will be very rare: for although he may not know it at the time, he will generally find that the man had been drinking, and it would have been policy on the part of the master not to have noticed it.

Natives often work exceedingly well under a white man to lead them, but it must be leading, not driving. The difficulty is for the farmer to get such a man, whilst to put two or three natives at a job far away from the homestead, where they will not be watched, is nearly tantamount to throwing away their day's labour. There seems to be something wanting in the native character which prevents him going steadily on when left to his own resources. We see it, not only with the ordinary labourer, but with the mechanic, trained at the missionary or other institution, where, whilst under a white foreman, his work might be equal to that of any journeyman ; but after he leaves the institution he seems to become utterly lost, and to be unable to make use of all he has learnt. That there are exceptions we are aware, but they are very, very rare. Whether the industry and perseverance of the white man are inherent, and the outcome of several generations of civilisation, and consequently cannot be expected in the native, or be the cause what it may, the farmer should never forget the fact, and endeavour to employ his labourers accordingly.

The usual scale of rations is 3lbs. of food a day for a single man, 4lbs. for a married man, and 5lbs. for a man with two wives, and all the thick milk on the farm divided amongst them. Where the farmer owns sheep, half of this is usually in meat, and the other half in mealies; where there are no sheep, half in meal and half in mealies, with an occasional change to a ration of meat. Where many cattle are kept, or the servants have cattle of their own, this ration is ample, and they will be constantly getting hangers-on ; but the quality of the rations should always be of the best, if the farmer would have contented labourers. It is also usual to give a piece of tobacco weekly, about a foot long.

Wages generally vary from 15s. to £2 a month. The best plan is to begin at a low rate, and raise those that are found worth it, or after they have been in your service a certain time. But it should never be forgotten that high wages will not tempt natives to remain under a master they do not like, unless they have got an eye to stealing some of his stock, and few natives can be trusted not to do this if they get the chance.

The greatest difficulty is generally when men first start farming. The native is very chary of going to a master until he knows something of him, but after he has been farming a few years, he establishes a certain connection, and a supply of relatives of those with him, or who have been with him, keep coming. And as long as food is scarce in Kaffirland he is fairly well off for labour; but let there be two or three good seasons when food gets plentiful, then is heard the cry from one end of the colony to the other of the scarcity of labour, and the farmers' hands are tied and all enterprise checked. The servants he has become off-handed and indifferent, and he becomes half worried to death to get along at all.

Very often native servants bring a few head of cattle with them. These make the most trustworthy servants, but as their cattle are often infected with lung-sickness, great care should be taken to isolate these cattle for the first two or three months.

As the native servants are not rationed with coffee

and sugar, or other luxuries, the opportunity of buying these things at a moderate rate should be given them. On a large farm by far the best plan is to have a little shop for them, where, besides groceries, they can obtain such things as boots, blankets, knives, handkerchiefs, cord clothing, calico, prints, pipes, &c. This need only be opened for an hour in the evening, and here the wages book should be kept, so that they can always hear how their account stands. This is an advantage which the natives fully appreciate : it gives them a direct interest in their wages, keeps them to some extent from spending their money in the canteens, and holds out a great inducement to the women to work when required. No license is necessary, so long as things are sold only to the employés. It costs the farmer nothing, as he can put on a per-centage sufficient to cover the expenses ; it encourages the natives to clothe themselves and their children to some extent, and is in every way an advantage.

Rows often take place on a farm about men not turning out in the morning, and the length of time they take at meals. Much of this can be avoided by having a good big bell, to be rung at the proper times. After a time the men get to like it, and much bother is saved, whilst it keeps master and all employed up to time.

Some years ago, being on a visit to Natal, and labour

being very scarce in the Cape Colony, we brought round
a few Indian coolie families on a three years' engage-
ment. They answered exceedingly well, and if labour
became again scarce we should get others. Only those
that have been ten years in Natal can leave it. For the
first five years after their immigration there they are
bound to the master who imported them ; for the next
five they are free to choose their own master, but cannot
leave Natal. After that they are free to leave, but
forfeit their right to a free passage back to India, which
they would otherwise be entitled to, and continue to be
entitled to as long as they remain in Natal, and report themselves every six months to the authorities.
The terms on which I got them, and could again get
them, were £2 a month wages, dating from the day they
left Natal, and a bonus of £9 at the end of the three
years for which they contracted, in lieu of the passage
to India they had forfeited. For rations they take meal
and rice with some fat, and a few pounds of meat once
a month, and a pound of split peas once a week. They
make exceedingly good herds for birds, and for looking
after little chicks ; they are useful also for gardening
work, but for hard work are not equal to the Kaffir.

The advisability of importing Coolies direct from
India, as they do in Natal, has often come before the
people in the Cape Colony. But it is not generally

known that the government in India only allow Coolies to emigrate to colonies that have complied with their conditions, and have been entered on their list of available fields for emigration. Their conditions are—that a Coolie office be established in the colony, with a gentleman at its head to act as a protector to them, that there is provision made by the government for their being medically visited, and that a stringent law be made to protect their interests.

# CHAPTER XXX.

## DAM-MAKING.

THE loss which is annually sustained in the country through the carrying away of dams is enormous, and yet nearly all this loss might be saved by a little knowledge and care in their construction. At all times dam-making is expensive and anxious work, generally costing far more than the farmer originally expected ; and in some cases, even where the dam stands and does not leak, it proves to be money wasted, from the drainage area being insufficient, or the silt that comes down the kloof quickly filling it up.

It is not our intention to write about large reservoirs intended for irrigation purposes, but about the small ordinary dams for supplying stock with water. With large dams across rivers, or anywhere where the works amount to a large undertaking intended for extensive irrigation, the farmer should long consider over his scheme, and give heed to the remarks of his neighbours before commencing. Many have been half ruined by prematurely commencing on an ill-digested scheme. The difficulties are great in a country like this, where

the veriest little dry bed for eleven months in the year
is a rushing torrent for the other month; and the capa-
city of the reservoir must be enormous if intended for
irrigation, unless it is fed by a constant stream or springs.

But where the farmer has fully satisfied himself by
some years' local experience that a large reservoir for
irrigation is feasible, that the land he purposes to irri-
gate is worth it, that the river runs often enough to
ensure his always having water at the time required, and
knows by experience the extraordinary height that these
apparently insignificant streams can rise, that the silt
and *débris* that come down are insignificant, and that
all the necessary conditions of success are there—he
should then have the site surveyed and full plans drawn
by an engineer before turning a sod—the cost of which
will be saved over and over again before the dam is
finished. If the engineer is a man of some years' colonial
experience, well and good; if not, far greater provision
for carrying off the surplus water will be required than
he will be likely to provide.

A dam for irrigation purposes that is dependent on
local surface drainage, no matter how large the drainage
area, will always prove a costly failure, excepting for
irrigating an acre or so of garden-ground immediately
behind it: the amount of water required and the length
of the droughts are too great.

Much was expected by many people on the passing
of the Irrigation Act, by which private persons could
borrow public money at a low rate of interest for irrigation works.   It was thought that the colony would be
able to produce its own food supply.   We never
thought so.   We considered that such people did not
sufficiently allow for the great difference in this
country, where the rainfall is uncertain and falls
quickly, and, from the mountainous formation of the
country, soon runs to the sea; whilst in countries that
have been pre-eminently successful with irrigation, such
as Lombardy, the country is flat, the streams run
nearly level with their banks, and take their rise in
snow-capped mountains, which keep up a constant and
moderate supply all the year round.

But with all these advantages which they possess, we
think it exceedingly doubtful whether, if they had to
construct their works in the present day and compete
with a free trade in corn, it could be made to pay.
These works were constructed when communication with
the rest of the world was slow and uncertain—before the
present great granaries of the world were discovered, or
steam-ships had turned the world into one vast market
for the interchange of those commodities which each
country was the best adapted to produce.

That a colony, that can grow its own breadstuffs, is in

a better way to become some day an independent nation, or would be less seriously affected in the event of England being involved in war with some naval power, must be admitted. But this is the political side of the question, which should be attended to by the government, by holding out every encouragement to the agriculturist. All we are here considering is the probable profit and loss to the individual farmer.

In a British colony, where the supply of bread-stuffs can be drawn from any part of the world, the circumstances must be very exceptionally favourable to enable a farmer to grow cereals by irrigation at a profit. If the works are anyways expensive, the interest on the capital and the extra labour of irrigating, coupled with the cramped nature of the cultivation, will exceed the cost of carriage from better-favoured countries, where the crops never fail, and where cultivation on an enormous scale and at a very cheap rate is practicable.

The farther inland irrigation works are constructed, the better their chance of paying, as then the foreign wheat is not only handicapped by the cost of ocean carriage, but of the far more expensive inland carriage. And since no cereals can be grown inland without irrigation, this expense of carriage is a constant item in its favour.

With carriage from the coast to the Diamond Fields at 21s. per hundred pounds, leaving out of the question the extra cost of grinding, there would be a premium of 2½d. per lb. on all wheat grown, to the credit of irrigation works up there, as against the same works on the coast, which would make all the difference between a handsome profit and a costly failure. But the Diamond Fields can often draw their bread-stuff supplies from the Free State and Basutoland, which can produce them in some seasons without irrigation, and being nearer, the carriage is less than from the coast.

The dams a farmer is most generally called upon to use his judgment in constructing, are ordinary stock dams that are required to hold sufficient water to last from one rain to another, for the stock to drink; they generally cost from £50 to £500. These are usually made across a kloof, or in a valley, the drainage into them being assisted by long furrows. For this sort of dam few would think of calling in an engineer, and there is no need to do so; but the farmer should bear in mind that no dam can be relied on as being water-tight when first made, unless a ditch, say, four feet wide, is first dug right along the centre of the site of the proposed embankment, and carried down to the rock or sound bottom, and is then filled in with puddled clay, and this puddling is carried on up the centre of

the embankment to the top. But this is often imprac-
ticable, from there being no water near the spot. The
farmer is then obliged to dispense with this puddled
core, and if the ground is of a good binding nature,
although it will be sure to leak at first, it may
eventually get quite water-tight.

The best dams, where there is no puddled core, are
those made with a scoop, as they then have a good
bevel, and the oxen tramp the bank solid in going up
and down with the scoop; but this sort of dam is
generally shallow, and cannot be made in all places.

The next best are those made with Scotch carts,
the working of which on the bank hardens it down,
though not so effectively as the scoop.

The worst are those made with wheelbarrows; the
earth falls so lightly that the subsidence, when the
water gets in it, is incredible to one inexperienced;
unless the bank was carried some feet higher than
would be eventually required, the water will go over
the top; and unless the material is thoroughly good,
the water will filter through it, and eventually melt
it away. The greater the slope of the inside of the
bank, and the more the stock are allowed to trample
over it, the better. The base should be the breadth
of the top of the bank, with at least two feet added
for every foot of height.

More dams are lost through the overflow being too small than by any other cause. A man looks at the run of water in the kloof, and makes his outlet accordingly, quite forgetting that the water there has got a straight flow, on an incline, and with an accumulated velocity; consequently, a very much larger amount of water will pass in the same space than will pass out of the overflow where the water is at rest, and generally flows out on a level. The same mistake is made where men talk of a spring, saying it would fill an inch pipe; whereas, a pipe lying level is one thing, and a pipe inclining down, say, to an angle of 45°, is quite another thing.

Another mistake that is commonly made is supposing the strength of the embankment depends on the distance the water is thrown back. This makes no difference whatever: the pressure entirely depends upon the depth. Thus, suppose an underground tank 10 ft. deep: it will not make the slightest difference to the strength required whether the tank is built 4 ft. square or 20 ft. square. Or, in other words, the weight of a column of water 1 in. square and 32 ft. high is 15 lbs., so that the pressure on the bottom of our tube will be 15 lbs.; but if we take a tube a foot square and 32 ft. high the pressure on any given square inch will only be 15 lbs., whilst if we take a

tube 16 ft. high the pressure on any given square inch
will only be 7½ lbs.

The most convenient way of paying for dam work
is by the cubic yard, the general price being from 1s. to
2s. a yard, the farmer finding carts, oxen, and drivers ;
but, of course, much depends on the nature of the soil.
The farmer should be careful not to make the mistake of
measuring the embankment instead of the excavation,
or he will pay dearly. Many farmers are deterred
from adopting payments by this plan, thinking from
the shape of the ground that it would be difficult to
measure, but when tried it is very simple.

Very much more might be done than is done by
looking for water under the surface. We have one
farm that was badly watered, but by simply noticing
five different places where some few rushes grew, and
sinking only four feet, we came on perennial springs in
every case, which all rose to the level of the ground, and
in some cases ran down the kloofs. Our experience
would teach us that wherever rushes grow in Karoo
country, there is a spring not far down, and that from
the appearance of the rush a very fair idea can be
formed of the depth it is down.

On three other spots where a hard round rush was
growing, we sank wells and got water in all at fourteen
feet, eighteen feet, and twenty-one feet respectively ; and

P

in two of them the water was perfectly fresh, though they were sunk in slate shale, where all the surface-water was brack, and much of it undrinkable.

Boring for Artesian wells has been much neglected, but we expect to see it come into vogue to a large extent in the next few years.

# CHAPTER XXXI.

## BUILDING.

" Fools build houses for wise men to live in " is an old saying with much truth in it, and expresses in a few words the experience of nearly every one who has built houses : before completion they too often cost nearly double the sum that was originally intended to be spent. Whilst, when it comes to selling them, they very rarely fetch anything like their cost.

Before Ostrich-farming began, a farm with a good house on it would scarcely let or sell at a higher figure than one with only a mere shanty. But now this is changed ; men know that good buildings, good sheds, &c., are essential to success, and they are quite ready, if these are adapted to the requirements, to give the full cost. In fact, it is hardly possible to let a farm to an Ostrich farmer if there are no buildings on it, unless some arrangement is made to allow the tenant for building.

Now, a young farmer is often in a fix. He knows he must have accommodation for his chicks if he would rear them—that slovenly, tumble-down buildings mean a slovenly farm in every way, In fact, the look of a

P 2

farmer's homestead, if he has lived there any length of time, will give you a very good idea of his farming powers.

But bricks and mortar are often a synonym for ruin, and it is only by bearing in mind that building to accommodate animals means laying one's money out to be reproduced, whilst building an unnecessarily good dwelling-house means money sunk not to return again, that regret in the future will be avoided.  To the farmer the quality of the sheds, stable, rearing-rooms, &c., should be of far greater moment than the quality and size of the dwelling-house.

When buildings of any extent are to be erected, by far the cheapest and best method is to have plans and specifications drawn by an architect, instead of the common plan with farmers of going to work on a half-formed idea, or letting some builder undertake to build a house of so many rooms, with possibly no stipulation as to the thickness of the walls, the amount of timber to be used in the roof, the size and quality of the windows and doors, or the hundred and one things that go to make up the difference in the quality of the house, and which, if not defined, must lead to disputes in which the farmer will be worsted, and will have to pay far more than he could have got it done for if there had been a full and definite contract in the first instance.

The architects charge 2½ per cent. for plans and specifications, and double this if they superintend the erection;
but this latter they cannot undertake in the country,
so that the first charge is all that is necessary, unless the
farmer for his own satisfaction pays them the charge
that is usually paid by the builder to get the list of
"quantities." This latter he would find it well worth
his while to do. But he should always arrange with the
architect that, in the event of any dispute with the
builder, he will come out for a fixed charge. This he
will generally do for two guineas a day and cart-
hire.

Although many farmers laugh at employing an
architect, it is astonishing how ignorant some are if you
ask them how thick their outside walls are to be, or
their partition walls, or whether they will use lime,
mortar, or dagga, or how they can best secure their
wall-plates, &c.

Although we say so strongly, employ an architect,
yet a man may want a shed or some outbuildings erected
where it would be needless to go to one, especially if it
is intended to do it by the yard, and not as a lump job;
so we will endeavour to give a few hints on building
which we think will be found useful. But before commencing to build, there is nothing like having a good
look at anything of the kind it is intended to erect on

the neighbouring farms, and taking notes of size, height, &c.

The common journeymen prices in the country run about as follows :—

| | | |
|---|---|---|
| 18-inch rough stone work ... | 4s. 6d. | per yard. |
| 14-inch brick work ... ... ... | 1s. 9d. | „ |
| 9-inch „ „ ... ... ... | 1s. 6d. | „ |
| Plastering both sides ... ... | 1s. 6d. | „ |
| Roofing ... 15s. per square of 100 super. feet. | | |

There is generally a difference of opinion between employer and employed as to whether these prices should include the mason finding rough labour, to mix mortar, &c. ; and who gives way much depends upon whether the man is anxious for a job or not. It is often settled by (in stone-work) the mason quarrying the stone, and the master then supplying all other labour; and in brick-work, the mason finding one man to hand him bricks and mortar, and the master all other labour.

In building with stone, it is always worth while to use lime mortar—lime in the proportion of one to three, and for plastering one to two. With brick the outside wall should never be less than fourteen inches thick, and for mortar dagga (that is, clay worked up the same as for making bricks,) answers very well ; but the joints must be raked out at least half an inch deep, or the plaster will soon fall off. The greatest difficulty is to get bricklayers to properly bed the bricks in mortar. The almost universal plan is to what they call " key " the ends, leaving the rest of the joints open, saying the next layer of mortar will run in ; but it does not, and the consequence is that in a heavy rain the wet comes through, and the heat. and cold are not kept out. If they are not watched they will not even key them, but put the bricks touching, with nothing between them, as they can then lay them much faster; but, of course, then there is nothing but the plaster to keep out the wet, and paper will never stay on the walls.

Many masons lay the foundation without any mortar between the stones, but it should not be allowed : if for no other reason than that it makes a perfect warren for mice.

In a country subject to such violent winds as this, great care should be taken to tye the wall plates fast. By far the best plan is to build a few long bolts into the wall, with a large washer in their ends, and bolt the plates down. Never make the mistake of using too light timber for the roof, or putting the rafters far apart.

A fall of one inch in a foot is enough to carry the water off and stop the rain driving up, in a roof covered with corrugated iron, but the higher the pitch the cooler the building will be ; whilst a flat roof in this country is only another name for being roasted alive.

In using cement for tanks or stoops, &c., unless the sand is very good it should be washed in tubs with two or three waters, and then for most purposes one part of cement to three of sand is strong enough ; but for tanks it should be one to two.

In making bricks on farms the clay is generally tramped with horses or natives, but it is seldom thoroughly done. The best ground is a fair clay, free of brack ; it is brack that ruins half the farm buildings. The price paid is generally 18s. a thousand for burnt bricks, the master finding the wood, and the maker all labour. But it is always best to stipulate only to pay for the bricks when counted out of the kiln, as if not, and if proper attention has not been paid to the burning, when the kiln is opened the number will be far short of what was expected. To burn them properly the man must be up all night to close the weather-eye of the kiln with the shifts of wind ; about three days and nights' burning will make a good kiln.

A little calculation will tell you how many bricks you require. Allow 130 bricks to a yard of fourteen-inch wall, and 90 bricks to a yard of nine-inch wall.

# CHAPTER XXXII.

## HIRING AND BUYING FARMS.

A FEW hints on the hiring and buying of farms will be found useful, especially as regards hiring, which up till lately was generally done without any written contract ; or when there was one it was often so vague that misunderstandings between the contracting parties was generally the result.

The first point upon which landlord and tenant generally differ is as regards who should pay the taxes on the farm, and as these are a considerable item, it should be the first question asked after the rent is named. The taxes consist of :—1st, Quit rent ; 2nd, House Duty ; 3rd, Divisional Road Rates ; 4th, Divisional Police Rates. The first is generally about £4 per annum, but if it is a farm that has been lately purchased from Government, as explained in the chapter on the Land Laws, it may be a hundred or more ; but this will, of course, have been ascertained. The second is on a sliding scale, according to the value of the house : on every hut or dwelling not over £100 in value, 10s. ; not exceeding £500 in value, £1 ; not exceeding £750,

£1 10s.; not exceeding £1,000, £2; and then rising £1 for every £250 in value, but in no case exceeding £10 per annum. The third and fourth are levied annually by the Divisional Councils, and vary according to their wants, being generally twopence in the pound on the value of the farm.

The annual rental of farms varies, of course, immensely, and it is hardly possible to lay down a rule as to what the rental should be. The nearest we can give is that it should be about eight per cent. on the Divisional Council valuation. These valuations are generally about two-thirds of what they would fetch in the market; but a farm that has been much improved by buildings and fences is never valued up to anything like the amount of the cost of the improvements, whilst bare land is often valued at its full market price. The Divisional Council valuations can always be obtained by inquiring at the Divisional Council office, which is in the town where the district magistrate resides.

The principal clauses that a landlord generally insists on in a farm lease are :—

1st. The rent payable every six months—sometimes required in advance.

2nd. All buildings and fences to be kept in present state of repair.

3rd. That no native squatters shall be allowed on the farm.

4th. That no portion of the farm shall be sub-let without owner's consent.

5th. That no wood or bush, or only a certain amount, shall be cut on the farm, excepting such as is required for farm use.

6th. By whom the taxes are to be paid.

The tenant should, if he can, get a clause inserted that any buildings or fences that he may erect should be taken by the owner at their value on the expiration of the lease, or, failing this, that he should have the right of removal. Landlords seldom agree to the former, but generally will to the latter, which answers the tenant's purpose well, but of course not equally as well as if the landlord would take them over at valuation.

If the tenant is a very cautious man, he will insist on a clause providing that if any building is burnt down it shall be rebuilt by the landlord.

On agricultural farms there will often be clauses regulating the amount of land to be cultivated ; and, where bush is scarce, a clause regulating the amount of bush-fencing that the tenant will be allowed to make.

The transferring of landed property is exceedingly simple at the Cape. Titles are all registered at the office of the "Register of Deeds," Cape Town, where all transfers are registered, and a deed of transfer is handed to the purchaser. Here, too, all mortgages are registered. If the land is purchased by auction, the purchaser always has to pay all expenses of advertising, auctioneer's fees, and transfer dues. The latter is 4 per cent. on the purchase money ; the auctioneer's fees are often 2½ per cent., the seller making a private bargain with the auctioneer to divide the amount, the auctioneer seldom actually getting more than 1 per cent. But this is sharp practice, and many sellers will only charge the purchaser the amount that the auctioneer is actually paid.

The usual terms of credit are :—all the above expenses to be paid on day of sale; first instalment in three months, next in six, and the others in twelve, eighteen, and twenty-four months ; the purchaser finding two approved sureties for the due fulfilment of the conditions. Transfer to be given after payment of the second instalment, the purchaser passing a mortgage bond as security for the payment of the remaining instalments. In private sales a certain amount down is often given in lieu of finding sureties.

Two-thirds is generally the outside that can be obtained on a mortgage bond ; and a purchaser should see his way to paying one-half of the amount, if he would not lay himself open to the liability of having his mortgage foreclosed, with the possibility of not being able to get somebody else to take the mortgage. But as long as the amount sought to be obtained on mortgage does not exceed one-half of the fair value of the property, it can always be obtained at from 7 to 8 per cent., and the mortgagor can feel perfectly easy.

When a farm is bought from the occupier he is generally permitted to continue in occupation from three to six months: this is to allow him time to purchase elsewhere, or to sell off, if he is giving up farming; the purchaser has the right of sending stock on the farm at once, and generally stipulates for the use of some part of the dwelling-house, and not to pay interest on the unpaid portion of the purchase-money till the seller clears out.

We need hardly caution an intending purchaser never to purchase without a thorough personal inspection, no matter how tempting an offer may be made him. One of the things he should be exceedingly careful about is that the water supply is really perennial, no matter how severe the drought; and a few judicious questions amongst the neighbours will prove of great value on this point. But when price and quality are found to be satisfactory, the intending purchaser should insist on seeing all corner and angle beacons, and should find out whether any of these are disputed by the neighbours, and if so, all particulars of the dispute, and had then better limit his offer to what he considers the farm worth, less the piece in dispute. Boundary lawsuits are exceedingly cumbersome and expensive processes, the costs generally exceeding the value of the land in dispute. Accompanying every title deed is a diagram of the land; and, if a recent one, all angles are marked on it, and it can be relied upon, and any missing corner-stone can easily be fixed again by a surveyor; but all the early surveys were most carelessly made, and no angles being given on the diagram it may be impossible to determine the true position of a missing beacon, and the diagram becomes little more than a fancy picture; but these farms are nearly always larger than the diagrams represent them.

Provided the angle beacons are standing and are undisputed, the line beacons can always be erected by the farmer, if he only provides himself with sufficient flags, no matter whether it goes through bush or over hills. He first takes a line of flags in a line that he thinks will strike the other corner, then seeing when he reaches that, how much he is out, takes another line, and so on till he hits the corner-stone, and having got the flags correct, proceeds to plant his stones along the line about fifty yards apart.

An excellent plan is to whitewash all beacon stones ; everybody on the farm then soon gets to know the boundaries, and unpleasantness between neighbours is often avoided.

# CHAPTER XXXIII.

ANNUALLY there go forth to the various British colonies hundreds of young Englishmen, most of them well principled, well brought up, and well educated, sound and robust, determined, and sent forth to carve out their own fortunes. For years Australia and New Zealand, with their attractive wool-growing pursuits, absorbed most of these; but now their attention is being largely turned to the Cape, especially in connection with Ostrich-farming, and justly so, for no colony offers a better field.

The bright, wild dreams of accumulating a rapid fortune in some pleasant manner, with little trouble to themselves, in some vague, undefined way, will soon be dispelled; and they will find that neither a decent living, a comfortable independence, nor a fortune, are to be had here, or anywhere else, without strenuous exertion, strict sobriety, command of temper, rectitude, and a power of turning their hands to whatever offers, and doing it with all their might. But these are just the qualities that distinguish the young Englishman above all others, and what has enabled him to build up such magnificent nations as the United States, the Canadas and Australasia, and is so rapidly developing South Africa.

That many fail, and instead of succeeding drop in the social scale, take to drink, or otherwise go to the dogs at the Cape as elsewhere, is but too true ; but this they would have done wherever they were, and is what they are daily doing in all the colonies. But there is no need that this should happen to a single one of them at the Cape, if they can only once get a footing. The first thing is to get some good introductions to leading men there, with a fair prospect of their either offering Juvenis employment, or finding some-one else who will do so.

The best immigrants are those who leave England between the ages of eighteen and twenty-five. After the latter age the mind seems to have been too fully imbued with fixed notions, and does not so readily embrace new phases of life, or adapt itself to new toils and pleasures. There is no special early training that gives one an advantage over another—certainly nothing in the shape of a training to English farming, which is far more likely to prove a disadvantage than otherwise, especially if it has been taught in a scientific manner. Juvenis has then not only to begin and learn every-

Q

thing, but he has to unlearn all he has learned. Men
that have had a training at English farming seem to be
the last to take in the total difference of the surrounding
circumstances, and to imagine that it is ignorance and
prejudice that makes old colonists keep mainly to the
old primitive grooves. And not till their capital is
gone, and they have become embittered by constant
failures, do they realise the fact that these men are
as shrewd, far-seeing, and enterprising as any in
England; but that experience has taught them that all
improved methods must come very gradually, and to be
successful must only advance at the same pace as the
available labour becomes gradually educated up, and
other surrounding circumstances of markets and roads
advance.

The spirit that goes a long way to make the difference between the young man that will make a successful
colonist and one that will not, is the habit of observation. That constant quick observation that never rests,
that notices every peculiarity in people and things: the
habit that would compel him, if he saw a man laying a
drain, to find out how deep it was, how the tiles were
laid, and the reasons why; or, if he passed some men
building a wall, would notice how the bricks were laid,
how the mortar was mixed, and all about it. In fact,
he must have the very opposite spirit to that of a

young friend of mine in a house I was staying at, and who told me they brewed their beer twice a year, but on my asking him how it was done, exclaimed, " O! I don't know.  I never bother myself to find out." Now, this young man had an idea of emigrating to the Cape, and on my telling him he hardly showed the spirit that was likely to make a successful colonist, wanted to know if he would have to brew at the Cape.  Most probably he would not, but the man that was too indifferent to learn how to brew beer when he had the chance would soon find that he did not know heaps of things he ought to know, and, at the best, would be very unlikely to strike out a new course and distinguish himself.  It was a wise man that remarked that some men would learn more in a walk down Oxford-street, than others by making a tour through Europe.

After a young man has determined to emigrate, if there is any time to elapse whilst friends are communicated with, he could not spend his time in any better way, if he is going to take up farming in a colony, than by going under a carpenter, and into a mechanical engineer's workshop, not to learn, but to work.  The knowledge he will pick up there will increase his value twofold as an assistant on a Cape farm.  At the same time, if he finds that steady manual work and soiling his hands with oil and grease are distasteful to him, he may be sure that he is not fitted to a colonial farmer's life; whilst a practical knowledge of the steam-engine, in a country where very little can be done without irrigation, will be of immense value to him all his life.

If it is intended he should follow mercantile pursuits, let him get a short training in a merchant's office or a bank, or anywhere where he can get a sharp taste that the world means work and not play. Anywhere at the Cape, outside of the purely English towns of Grahamstown, Port Elizabeth, King William's Town and the Diamond Fields, a knowledge of the Cape patois Dutch is an indispensable essential in business; and anyone who can speak the high Dutch as spoken in Holland, or even German, will quickly pick up Cape Dutch.

Much money is often wasted in providing young men with an expensive outfit, which had much better have been laid by as a little capital. Much of the clothing taken is of too warm a nature, and suitable clothing could have been bought nearly as cheap at the Cape, as required. Whilst the money spent on guns, revolvers, &c., would have been much better laid out on a thoroughly good tool-chest; and the parent, in giving him the guns, has been rather encouraging him in the idea that life is going to be made up of shooting and sport, instead of—as he will find it—mostly hard work. For clothing, all that is wanted is a good-sized portmanteau, containing the ordinary outfit of a gentleman, with a few extra flannel shirts and socks.

And now, before taking leave of our book, can we say a few words that may help you young Englishmen, to whom my heart often yearns, as I see you so full of life and hope starting on your journey through life? Bear in mind that the day you step on board the steamer, leaving father and mother, or dear friends who have thought for and screened you, far more than you have known, from the many evils that so particularly attend you at your time of life, that from that moment you begin the fight single-handed. That one of the first great evils, the scourge of drinking, will meet you at once—the rock that wrecks and utterly blights the lives of thousands of you. Make up your mind at once on the subject, and let it be never to drink any intoxicating liquors, saving at meal-time, unless under most exceptional circumstances, and keep to it firmly, but quietly. You may have seen cases of ruin by drink in England, but you can know nothing of the fearful curse it is in all the colonies; and most of it brought about by a silly habit young men have of asking each other to take a liquor when neither want it; it is done to wile away a few minutes, or to appear friendly, and is accepted by the other for fear he should appear churlish. But do not be misled : if your friend is worth having he will not think you churlish, and in his inner mind will be glad that you saved him the expense, and drinking what he knew he would be better without. Remember it is to the passage out on board the steamer that many a miserable, broken-down, pitiable object can trace his fall.

Another great stumbling-block is often encountered on board the steamer—gambling. This is indulged in by some men on every steamer; and where it is wealthy men gambling amongst themselves, the whole stakes they play for being a matter of indifference, there is no harm done; the harm is where a man stakes what he cannot afford to lose with indifference. In all steamers there is generally a daily wager on the distance the ship will run. It often begins innocently enough, and Juvenis thinks there is no harm in it, and joins in, and having made a loss, goes on, in the hopes of retrieving, instead of at once stopping.

Arrived in the colony, you will find that a farming life is very different to life in England—that it is not all roses, but neither is it all thorns. Its solitariness is its worst feature. Farms are large, and half one's neighbours are often cut off by rivers that are constantly impassable, or by high hills that make it a

day's work to visit them; and it is generally a case
of having said good-bye to cricket, lawn tennis,
billiards, and other amusements that are so attractive
in early life.   But against these we have the healthy
open life, in most parts good shooting, any amount of
riding, and above all, the most perfect independence to
be had anywhere in the world.   In England the landed
gentry are always envied for the independence their
position gives them, but their independence is hampered
by numerous conventionalities of which the well-to-do
Cape farmer is independent; whilst if he has had
the good sense when he left England to determine that
the Cape should be his home for good, he will soon
find his interest in colonial institutions and politics
growing upon him, and himself possessed of nearly
all the advantages in another sphere that the English
landed gentleman has in his.   No greater mistake is
ever made than that made by the man who emigrates to
a colony simply with the idea of grubbing money
together to enable him to return to England and spend
it in his old age.   But few succeed till so many years
have passed that their zest for English amusements and
ways has gone, and their English friends and relations
have changed so much that they seem almost as
strangers.

To struggle to amass wealth simply with the idea

to return and spend it in idleness is selfish and un-ennobling, making the getting it mere drudgery, and the spending it a disappointment ; but to get it by honest means, by extra intelligence and industry, with the object of starting one's children well in the world, and to acquire influence and a voice in the land of one's adoption, and to found a family name in a country such as the Cape, is an object worthy of any man's ambition, and one that will bring no disappointment in the realising—will hold out a high stimulant to the strictest honesty and uprightness, whilst proving a benefit to all with whom he is thrown in contact.

Reader, if you are such an one as this chapter is addressed to—young, strong, self-reliant, and can see your way to get a footing at the Cape in Ostrich-farming—go forth. The world is before you, the limit to what you may do or become is unbounded : on yourself it will depend. A bed of roses you will not find it : often you will sigh for old associations and friends, and often your lot may look dark; but when such is the case, instead of looking on the dark side, look at what most of your schoolfellows are doing : tied down to an office desk to drudge on with scarcely any prospect in front of them, beyond, at the best, securing a competency for themselves, and in due course being buried and forgotten; whilst you have a grand field before you where, by your discoveries or inventions, or other unknown powers within you, you may develope new industries, or discover mineral wealths, and turn the tide of prosperity on the country of your adoption that will send your name down to posterity as a great benefactor.

# ADDENDUM.

## International Exhibition, Philadelphia, 1876.

---

THE United States Centennial Commission has examined the Report of the Judges, and accepted the following reasons, and decreed an Award in conformity therewith :—

*Philadelphia, January 10th, 1877.*

### REPORT ON AWARDS.

*Product*—Ostrich Incubating Machine.

*Name and address of Exhibitor*—A. DOUGLASS, Heatherton Towers, Grahamstown, Cape of Good Hope.

The undersigned, having examined the product herein described, respectfully recommend the same to the United States Centennial Commission for Award, for the following reasons, viz. :—

As an apparatus for hatching out Ostrich Eggs in a simple and efficient manner, and for helping the young during the critical period of their early life :

The invention and use of this apparatus, and the treatment of the eggs and young of the Ostrich by Mr. Douglass, have added a most important industry to the world; and in addition to averting the threatened extermination of this species, have greatly multiplied its numbers, and increased the supply of its feathers for commercial purposes. These can now be taken, year by year, from the same (domesticated) bird, instead of involving its destruction for a single crop.

(*Signature of the Judge*) SPENCER F. BAIRD.

*Approval of Group Judges.*

| | |
|---|---|
| EDWARD CONLEY. | COLEMAN SEKERS. |
| B. F. BRITTON. | H. K. OLIVER. |
| J. FRITZ. | JAMES L. CLAGHORN. |
| CHARLES STAPLES, Jun. | HENRY H. SMITH. |

A true copy of the Record.
FRANCIS A. WALKER,
*Chief of the Bureau of Awards.*

Given by the authority of the United States Centennial Commission.
A. T. GRAHAM, *Director General.*
J. L. CAMPBELL, *Secretary.*
J. R. HAWLEY, *President.*

www.ingramcontent.com/pod-product-compliance
Lightning Source LLC
Chambersburg PA
CBHW030628030726
47497CB00006B/1694